VEGAN

IN THE HOUSE

VEGAN

IN THE HOUSE

Consultant Heather Whinney

Editors Laura Bithell,
Anna Cheifetz, Helena Caldon

US Editor Kayla Dugger

Designers Steve Marsden,
Alison Gardner, Vanessa Hamilton

Jacket Designer Nicola Powling

Producer, Pre-production Heather Blagden

Producer Igrain Roberts

Indexer Michele Moody

Managing Editor Dawn Henderson

Managing Art Editor Alison Donovan

Art Director Maxine Pedliham

Publisher Mary-Clare Jerram

First American Edition, 2019
Published in the United States by DK Publishing
345 Hudson Street, New York, New York 10014

A catalog record for this book is available from the
Library of Congress.
ISBN 978-1-4654-8039-2

Printed and bound in China

A WORLD OF IDEAS:
SEE ALL THERE IS TO KNOW

www.dk.com

CONTENTS

INTRODUCTION

It is increasingly common to live in a house in which at least one person is vegan. Veganism is steadily becoming one of the most popular diets worldwide, with people adopting a plant-based diet for reasons varying from environmental and animal welfare concerns to personal health. Vegans exclude all animal products from their diet—this includes meat, fish, eggs, and dairy, but also any product with an ingredient derived from animals. Some of these, such as certain brands of orange juice, may surprise you!

If you or a family member has decided to make the switch, it's natural to have a few concerns. You may worry about maintaining a balanced diet or about finding somewhere to eat out. If it's your child who has decided to go vegan, perhaps you're worried they won't get enough calcium or iron. The introduction pages are written with this in mind—they tackle the myths of veganism, suggest the best animal product substitutes, provide guidance on shopping and storing, and give you a full understanding of the nutrients the body needs and how to source these through a plant-based diet. "The good stuff" boxes on many recipes offer useful nutritional information and highlight the health benefits of each dish.

From hearty, healthy main dishes to delicious but not-so-naughty desserts, the 100-plus recipes in this book are designed to cover everyone's wants and needs. It is often easier to make the change to veganism gradually, and not everyone in the household may be following the same diet. The "flex it" boxes are written for convenience and flexibility, so home-cooked meals can be eaten by vegetarians, pescatarians, meat-eaters, and flexitarians with just a few tweaks and additions to the recipes.

Eating a balanced diet is vitally important for all of us, so a switch to veganism for one member of the household can be a good time to reconsider the whole family's eating habits. Discover the powerful potential of plant-based foods to take center stage and to keep the whole household happy and well fed.

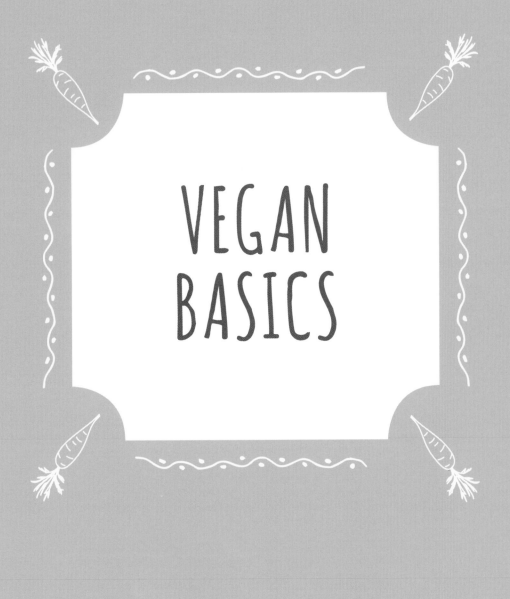

VEGAN BASICS

MYTH-BUSTING

Adopting a vegan diet is a personal choice and is often based on nutrition, animal welfare, or the environment. As with many alternative dietary choices, there are some common misconceptions. Here, the top myths that surround veganism are dispelled.

A VEGAN DIET IS EXPENSIVE!

IT DOESN'T HAVE TO BE ... As with all diets, the cost greatly depends on how much you cook from scratch. The most efficient way to economize is to plan your weekly cooking and shop accordingly. Expensive convenience foods can be avoided. Instead, rely on fresh produce. You will actually be saving money by not buying meat and fish, as they can be expensive. Instead, gradually build up a pantry of dried goods. This means you can always make a meal on a budget.

IT'S NOT HEALTHY!

YES, IT CAN BE ... What constitutes healthy for anyone is a varied and broad diet, and many nonvegan diets may be very unhealthy if nutrition isn't considered. Vegans have the same nutritional needs as everyone else, so think about balance, eating a variety of colors, and ensuring you get enough of all the food groups. Protein is often a big worry, as traditionally this comes from chicken, meat, fish, and dairy—but there are plenty of plant-based sources, too.

VEGANS ARE ALWAYS TIRED

NO, THEY AREN'T ... As long as you don't load up on convenience foods, you will have plenty of energy. You just need to ensure you are getting any nutrients typically found in animal products, such as calcium and iron, from other sources. Most nutrients can be easily replaced by plant-based sources, and there are also lots of fortified products available.

VEGAN FOOD IS BORING

NO, IT ISN'T ... People tend to think that a vegan diet consists of kale and salads. The reality is that a plant-based diet can be full of extremely tasty and varied food. It's best to focus on getting a range of fruits, vegetables, and other plant-based foods into your diet rather than think about what you'll be cutting out. The key is to experiment with flavors so your palate is sated; this way, you won't feel like something is missing. Season your food well to enhance the flavors.

THE FOOD IS DIFFICULT TO PREPARE!

IT CERTAINLY ISN'T ... Vegan cooking can actually be easier than cooking with meat, fish, or dairy, as vegetables are very forgiving and adaptable. Cooking techniques are also largely the same, making the transition easy. Roasting, griddling, and barbecuing will draw out the best flavors from some vegetables, and grilling, poaching, or steaming can be used for fresher flavors. The only difficulty really lies in being adventurous, but this can be taken slowly. Start by adapting nostalgic comfort foods and gradually build up your recipe repertoire.

IT'S IMPOSSIBLE TO EAT OUT!

NOT ANYMORE ... Eating out is no longer a problem, as many places now offer a vegan option and there are increasing numbers of purely vegan restaurants. Many world cuisines have dishes that are traditionally vegan or can be easily adapted. Chinese restaurants have lots of tofu and vegetable dishes to choose from, but be on the alert for hidden fish-based pastes and sauces—it is always wise to ask. Indian cuisine often has lentil or vegetable specialities, but watch out for ghee and yogurt used in the cooking. Many Thai dishes are vegan, but ask, as some dishes contain hidden scrambled eggs!

THE BALANCED VEGAN DIET

For new vegans, one major concern is ensuring you still get the nutrients you need. Vegans have the same basic nutritional needs as everyone else, but they need to adjust the proportions of each food group. The key is balancing everything so you remain strong, energized, and in good health. This means making sense of what a healthy vegan meal is comprised of and building up a nourishing repertoire of dishes.

EVERYONE'S DAILY NEEDS

NUTRITION NEEDS VARY depending on your sex, size, age, and activity levels. So as individuals, we all have varying requirements for energy and nutrients. This chart is a general guide to daily recommended amounts per day for a moderately active adult, whether following a vegan diet or not.

	MEN	WOMEN
ENERGY (KCAL)	2,500	2,000
PROTEIN (g)	55	50
CARBOHYDRATES (g)	300	260
SUGAR (g)	120	90
FAT (g)	95	70
SATURATED FAT (g)	30	20
SALT (g)	6	6

30g fiber a day is recommended by health experts

! DRINK 6–8 CUPS OR GLASSES OF WATER PER DAY

Aim to eat 3–4 servings of fruit daily.

1 serving = 1 piece or about 3oz (85g)

FRUITS

These include avocados, nuts, and dairy substitutes such as almond and soy. Don't overdo it.

1 serving = ⅓ cup of nuts, ½ avocado

HIGH-FAT WHOLE FOODS

THE VEGAN PYRAMID

THIS MODIFIED, VEGAN VERSION of the food group pyramid is a great starting point for getting balance and variety into a plant-based diet. It is only a general guide, so don't worry if you can't get all of the food groups in every day—sometimes this may not be practical if you're busy or you have other foods to finish in the refrigerator. As long as you practice eating a variety of different healthy foods, it will all balance out over the week.

Broccoli, cabbage, spinach, and kale are good examples. Eat at least 2–3 servings daily.

1 serving = 2¾ cups uncooked

LEAFY GREENS

These protein-packed foods include beans, peas, and lentils. Eat 2–3 servings per day.

1 serving = palm of your hand, about ⅔ cup

LEGUMES

Brown rice, quinoa, buckwheat, barley, farro, whole-grain pasta, and sprouted grains are good choices. Always choose unrefined carbs, as these are high in fiber. Eat 5 or more servings per day.

1 serving = 1 tbsp grains or 1 slice of whole-wheat bread

WHOLE GRAINS

You can't eat too many veggies! Eat as many different colors as possible each day.

VEGETABLES

KEY MACRONUTRIENTS

Macronutrients are the nutrients needed in large amounts by the body to provide the bulk of your energy—they are the caloric building blocks of food. They are divided into fat, carbohydrates, and protein (see pp.12–13 for the recommended daily amounts of each). Many vegans worry about protein, as this traditionally comes from meat, fish, and dairy, but there are plenty of great plant-based sources, too.

FAT

A CERTAIN AMOUNT OF FAT is essential for the body to function, and it helps it absorb vitamins A, D, and E. Unhealthy saturated fats are mainly derived from animal products, so you're benefiting from cutting these out, but the healthier unsaturated fats play an important part in a healthy vegan diet. Seeds and nuts are a great source of unsaturated fats, such as the healthy fatty acid omega-3. The body doesn't need a huge amount of fat, so watch your intake of fatty foods—even the healthy ones!

GOOD PLANT-BASED SOURCES OF UNSATURATED FATS

Healthy fats are found in foods such as avocados, almonds, walnuts, cashews, Brazil nuts, pumpkin seeds, chia seeds, olive oil, winter squash, leafy greens, and members of the cabbage family.

CARBOHYDRATES

CARBOHYDRATES ARE the main energy source for our body, so it is necessary to include them to avoid fatigue and anxiety. They are fairly easy to come by in a vegan diet; the trick is to stick to eating the healthiest sources. You don't have to load up on bread and potatoes—many fruits, vegetables, and whole grains are carbs, too.

GOOD PLANT-BASED SOURCES OF CARBS

Fruits and vegetables such as bananas, broccoli, apples, sweet potatoes, leafy greens, carrots, figs, and squash. Whole grains such as wild rice, whole-wheat rice, and oats.

PROTEIN

PROTEIN BUILDS MUSCLE, cells, and tissue and produces hormones and antibodies. It is made up of 20 amino acids, of which nine are essential, as we can't make these ourselves. As a vegan, you need to make sure to eat a variety of different protein sources to get all the amino acids your body needs. Below are some of the best plant-based sources.

GRAINS

- BUCKWHEAT 1 cup provides 22.5g of protein.
- COOKED WILD RICE 1⅛ cups provides 6.5g of protein.
- QUINOA 1 cup provides 8g of protein.

SEEDS

- CHIA SEEDS 2 tbsp provides 4g of protein.
- HEMP SEEDS 3 tbsp provides 10g of protein.

LEGUMES

- COOKED BLACK BEANS A ¼-cup serving will provide 7.5g protein and is packed with B6. Good for slow-releasing energy.
- COOKED ORGANIC EDAMAME BEANS A 1 tbsp serving provides high-quality protein with all the essential amino acids. Eating 1¼ cups will provide you with about 22g of protein, nearly half the daily recommended amount.
- LENTILS A ½-cup serving will provide 9g protein. As lentils are high in fiber and low in calories, they are good for slow-releasing energy.
- ORGANIC TEMPEH A 2½oz (75g) serving provides 16g of protein.
- ORGANIC TOFU A 2½oz (5g) serving will provide 8-15g of protein. This is a similar protein content to chicken. It will keep you full for hours. Spreadable varieties taste good on oatcakes.
- PEANUT BUTTER 2 tbsp will provide 7g of protein.
- PEANUTS A ½-cup serving will provide 7g of protein. Great for snacking on.

VITAL VITAMINS

A group of micronutrients found in different types of food, vitamins are essential for our body's growth, vitality, and general well-being. Most of these can be gained from a balanced vegan diet, although you may need supplement B12 and D. The Bs and vitamin C need to be consumed each day, as the body cannot store them. The wheel highlights the function of each vitamin and the best sources for vegans.

Energy production; hair, skin, and nail health
- GREEN PEAS
- SQUASH
- BEANS
- SEEDS
- ASPARAGUS

Energy production; hair, skin, and nail health
- ARTICHOKES
- AVOCADOS
- CURRANTS
- MUSHROOMS
- NUTS

Energy production; hair, skin, and nail health
- YEAST
- PEANUTS
- CHILI POWDER
- SEITAN
- BUCKWHEAT

Energy production; hair, skin, and nail health
- SWEET POTATOES
- CARROTS
- PUMPKINS
- BUTTERNUT SQUASH
- SPINACH

Blood clotting to help heal wounds
- KALE
- SPINACH
- BRUSSELS SPROUTS
- SWISS CHARD
- GREEN BEANS

Protection from free radicals (antioxidant)
- SUNFLOWER OIL
- PEANUTS
- HAZELNUTS
- ALMONDS
- SUNFLOWER SEEDS

Calcium absorption, strong bones and teeth, muscle health
- FORTIFIED CEREALS
- FORTIFIED PLANT-BASED MILK
- MUSHROOMS
- VITAMIN D SUPPLEMENTS
- SUNSHINE!

Iron absorption, protection from free radicals
- STRAWBERRIES
- ORANGES
- BROCCOLI
- PEPPERS
- TOMATOES

Nerve and blood cell health, DNA creation
- B12 SUPPLEMENTS
- FORTIFIED VEGAN MILK AND YOGURT
- FORTIFIED CEREAL

A
B1
B2
B3
B5
B6
B7
B9
B12
C
D
E
K

16   VEGAN BASICS

VITAMINS AND MINERALS

Vitamins and minerals are the two types of micronutrients. They are needed in smaller amounts than macronutrients but are equally as important to our well-being. They help to regulate metabolism, the heart, and bone density.

Energy production; hair, skin, and nail health

TAHINI • BROCCOLI
SUNFLOWER SEEDS
YEAST

Detoxification, cognitive function, curing anemia

SOY PRODUCTS
BANANAS
FIGS
WATERMELON
PEANUT BUTTER

Energy production, blood sugar reduction, metabolism

ALMONDS
CHIA SEEDS
PEANUTS
SWEET POTATOES
OATS

Brain development, red blood cell health

SPINACH
TOMATOES • BEANS
LENTILS • LETTUCE

MUST-HAVE MINERALS

Minerals help with bone and tooth formation, blood coagulation, and muscle contraction. They are divided into macro minerals and trace minerals. Your body needs macro minerals in much larger amounts than trace minerals. As long as you eat a varied, balanced, plant-based diet, you'll get plenty of most minerals. However, there are a few exceptions you should watch out for.

MACRO MINERALS

calcium, chlorine, magnesium, phosphorus, potassium, sodium, and sulfur.

CALCIUM A big worry for some when not consuming dairy is "Where will my calcium come from?" Calcium can be found in dark leafy greens, fortified plant milk, soy products, nuts, and seeds, as well as some fruit, such as blackberries, oranges, and figs.

TRACE MINERALS

chromium, cobalt, copper, fluorine, iodine, iron, manganese, molybdenum, selenium, and zinc.

IRON As red meat is the most common source of iron, vegans need to look elsewhere for good plant-based sources. There are plenty of iron-rich vegan options, such as lentils, chickpeas, beans, tofu, cashews, spinach, ground linseed, kale, raisins, fortified breakfast cereal, and quinoa.

IODINE Our body needs iodine to make thyroid hormones. Often sourced from dairy, vegan milk options don't contain adequate levels of it, so you need to include iodine-rich foods in your diet. Cranberries or cranberry juice, strawberries, navy and lima beans, potatoes baked in skins, and seaweed are all good sources.

VEGAN SUBSTITUTES

It can be overwhelming at first to embark on a plant-based diet, but with all the substitutes that are available, the transition can be made much simpler. Easy vegan swaps can now be found for most familiar foods in supermarkets, making the weekly grocery shopping less intimidating and the cooking far easier.

MILK

For many new vegans, finding a good milk alternative is the most important swap. The decision is often down to taste preferences, but it is also worth comparing the nutritional benefits of plant-based milks.

ALMOND MILK	Almond milk is a popular choice for flavor. It is usually fortified with calcium, but is not a great source of protein or fiber. Best for overall cooking—but the flavor can overpower in baking.
COCONUT MILK	Coconut milk is lower in calories than other plant-based milks, but it is not naturally nutritionally packed unless it is fortified. It contains virtually no protein.
OAT MILK	Oat milk is the best choice for fiber, but low in protein and high in carbohydrates and calories. It has a decent amount of calcium and iron and naturally contains B vitamins that soy and almond milk don't. It is a good option for those with soy or nut allergies and good for baking.
SOY MILK	Soy milk is the most protein-rich option, and nutritionally the most similar to cow milk. However, it doesn't contain huge amounts of calcium, iodine, or B vitamins unless added. Drink sparingly if you already eat a lot of other soy products. Soy milk makes the best latte!

BUTTER

Plant-based margarine can be substituted weight for weight in recipes. Olive-oil-based versions are good for shallow frying and spreading and are lower in calories than other margarines. Soy spread is also good for general cooking, and sunflower spread works well for baking.

YOGURT

Vegan soy yogurt is a great dairy yogurt alternative; it also tends to react in a similar way when cooking. Coconut yogurt supplies several key vitamins and minerals and can have live and active cultures just like milk-based yogurts.

CHEESE

Nutritional yeast is a good substitute, especially for baking, as it offers a savory cheese flavor and it is rich in B vitamins. Vegan versions of most cheeses are also now widely available. It's probably best to try out a few different types and brands, as it's all down to personal taste.

EGGS

Eggs are invaluable for baking, but the starchy water from canned chickpeas and beans (aquafaba) is full of protein and can be used as the perfect egg replacement. It has emulsifying, binding, foaming, and thickening properties and performs as egg whites do when whipped—making it the ideal ingredient to make meringues. It is best to use the water straight from the can of chickpeas. A regular 14fl oz (400ml) can has about 12 tbsp of aquafaba. As a rule of thumb, 3 tbsp of aquafaba = 1 whole egg and 2 tbsp = 1 egg white.

HONEY

Replacing honey in a recipe is fairly simple. You can generally swap the honey quantity for the same amount of agave, which is a concentrated sweetener with a similar texture to honey. Maple syrup also makes a good swap, as it has a similar texture and is good for drizzling. Maple syrup has a slightly stronger flavor than agave, and the really good stuff can be quite expensive, but a little goes a long way.

MEAT

Seitan, tempeh, and tofu are the major meat alternatives, all of which can be bought in their natural form or marinated with added flavors. Many recipes will also replace meat with filling grains, pulses, and nuts.

SEITAN	Seitan is a nonsoy product. Its texture and its ability to absorb flavors make it a good meat substitute. It is made by washing wheat flour dough with water until all the starch has been removed. This leaves the dense, elastic gluten which can be baked, sautéed, steamed, or stewed. It is high in protein and low in calories, but can't be eaten by anyone with wheat allergies or following a gluten-free diet.
TEMPEH	Tempeh is made by fermenting soybeans, a process that ups the protein content to rival meat. Tempeh is even healthier than tofu, as the fermentation helps to break down anti-nutrients found in soybeans, making its proteins more digestible. It is also high in vitamins B5, B6, B3, and B2. Tempeh is good for grilling, frying, and roasting and makes a great bacon substitute.
TOFU	Tofu is also called bean curd. It is made by curdling and pressing soy milk (made from soybeans) into the blocks of tofu that you can buy. It is low in fat and calories and high in protein and amino acids. Firm tofu is good for using in stir-fries and soups, as it keeps its structure.

TIPS FOR MAKING THE SWITCH

The switch to a plant-based diet can be smooth sailing, but to make sure it works for you, it needs to fit into your lifestyle. You may need more time to prep main meals and snacks, investigate nutrition, and change your shopping habits. It doesn't have to be all or nothing—you can make changes at your own pace. Whatever the transition, eating a plant-based diet will eventually become a natural part of your life.

1
BUY WHOLE FOODS

Team up with friends and order in bulk to save money. Decant whole foods into jars and containers and use them frequently in your favorite recipes.

2
EDUCATE YOURSELF

This will give you the motivation and conviction to make the changes. It will also help you answer any questions people may ask about your new diet.

3
BE INSPIRED

Read up on recipes and learn as much as you can about cooking your favorite vegan meals. Why not try recipe swaps with friends and family?

4
PLAN AHEAD

If dishes for mealtimes are planned, it will save on time, money, and energy. It will also stop you grabbing an emergency fast-food meal or a processed snack.

5 BATCH COOK

Cook one for now and one for the freezer. This will free up time when the family is busy or when you're too tired to start cooking a big meal.

6 MAKE FAMILY FAVORITES

Learn to make healthy vegan versions of favorite fast foods or junk foods, such as burgers, Chinese food, or pies.

7 TAKE A SUPPLEMENT

It will offer reassurance that you are getting the nutrients you need.

8 DRINK FLUIDS

Healthy fluids such as water and herbal teas are great for keeping you hydrated and alleviating hunger pangs— we are often thirsty when we think we are hungry!

9 EXPERIMENT

Get creative in the kitchen as much as you can, trying new flavor combinations and cooking methods. This keeps a vegan diet exciting. Don't be afraid of failures!

10 FILL THE FRIDGE

Make sure your refrigerator is packed with healthy vegan snacks, and remove any overprocessed foods to avoid temptation.

THE YOUNG VEGAN

A vegan diet can be suitable for all ages, but as with any restrictive diet, it is wise to consult a dietician or nutritionist before making the transition so no compromises are made and daily nutritional targets are met. It is ideal for children to learn about diet as early on as possible so they can continue to make informed, healthy choices as they get older.

GROWING CHILDREN

CHILDREN GROW RAPIDLY from toddler to 12, so they need a diet that provides adequate amounts of protein to calorie ratio for energy and development. The best thing you can do for your vegan children is to introduce them to as many flavors and textures as early on as you can, which will develop the palate so they become more adventurous. Children eating a healthy plant-based diet will be far more nourished than children growing up on junk food, but in order to provide this, you need to be mindful of any particularly important nutrients or specific adjustments for kids.

VITAMIN D
Children need a lot of vitamin D, the sunshine vitamin, for healthy bone growth. Make sure they get plenty from fortified cereals.

IRON
Make sure your child gets enough iron from a plant-based diet. Iron gives red blood cells the "strength" to carry oxygen in the body, which is vital for children's growth.

FIBRE
Vegan diets can be too high in fiber for young children, so they tend to feel completely full before they've eaten enough nutrients. Try giving them some white bread, pasta, and rice instead of brown versions.

CALCIUM
Calcium is vital for growing bones and teeth. This typically comes from dairy products, but many plant-based alternatives and cereals are fortified with calcium.

FUEL FOR TEENAGERS

TEENS NEED TO EAT at least three nutritious meals a day, a couple of healthy snacks, and plenty of water. Teenage boys need 2,500 calories a day and girls 2,000. Skipping meals only leads to bad eating habits and unhealthy snacking. Food also plays a vital role in concentration, so teens need to eat regularly to keep blood sugars from dropping and the brain from becoming foggy. They should fill up on nutrient-dense whole foods that will help the body thrive physically and mentally. There are some nutrients that you need more of as you go into your teenage years.

5 QUICK ENERGY BOOSTS FOR KIDS

- TROPICAL FRUIT SMOOTHIE BOWL (pp.40-41)
- PEANUT BUTTER & BANANA BALLS (pp.54-55)
- LEMONY SPINACH HUMMUS (pp.64-65)
- CHICKPEA BITES (p.66)
- MUNG BEAN GUACAMOLE (pp.70-71)

IRON

The need for iron increases in teenagers as their muscle mass increases and blood volume expands. It is recommended that teenage boys get on average 11 milligrams of iron a day and girls get 15 milligrams a day. Not getting enough iron can lead to anemia, which will result in fatigue, headaches and light-headedness, and an inability to concentrate.

PROTEIN

Protein requirements increase for teens because of metabolic changes, growth spurts, and high activity. Their needs should be met if they eat a varied diet with plenty of legumes, seeds, and whole grains.

CALCIUM

Calcium is especially important for teens because it's a period of major growth spurts. Make sure teens are consuming enough calcium to prevent the future risk of osteoporosis—consuming adequate calcium during the teenage years reduces the risk of brittle bones later in life.

VITAMIN C

It is a good idea for teens to be particularly careful to eat foods rich in vitamin C as part of their meals, as this vitamin helps the body absorb more iron.

SHOPPING FOR VEGAN FOODS

Whether you or your family are transitioning into eating a wholly plant-based diet or you are going to do it a few steps at a time, your shopping habits will begin to change. If you are strapped for time, it makes sense to research ahead of supermarket trips so time isn't wasted.

LABEL READING

IT'S EASY TO shop for fresh fruits and vegetables, but it can get tricky with non-perishable foods. Many products now clearly state if they are vegan, but it is wise to know the nonvegan sneaky ingredients that might trip you up.

- **ALBUMEN** comes from eggs.
- **ASPIC** comes from clarified meat or fish or from gelatin.
- **CASEIN** is milk protein.
- **COD LIVER OIL** comes from a cod's liver.
- **COLLAGEN** comes from the skin, bones, or connective tissue of animals.
- **DAIRY AND EGGS** are allergens, so these will be clearly stated on the label and any by-products will be highlighted.
- **E NUMBERS** are food additives and may contain things like cochineal (a dye made from beetles).
- **ELASTIN** is similar to collagen but comes from the neck ligaments of cows.
- **GELATIN** is derived from the boiled bones, skin, and ligaments of cows or pigs.
- **HONEY** is produced by bees.

- **ISINGLASS** comes from the bladder of fish (may be used in refining wine and beer).
- **KERATIN** comes from the skin, bones, or connective tissue of animals.
- **LACTOSE** is a milk sugar.
- **LARD/TALLOW** is animal fat.
- **PEPSIN** comes from a pig's stomach.
- **PROPOLIS** is used by bees to make their hives.
- **ROYAL JELLY** is a secretion from the honey bee.
- **SHELLAC** comes from the body of a female insect.
- **VITAMIN D3** is sometimes derived from fish liver or sheep's wool (lanolin). It can be vegan if made from lichen. Always check the label!
- **WHEY** is a milk by-product.

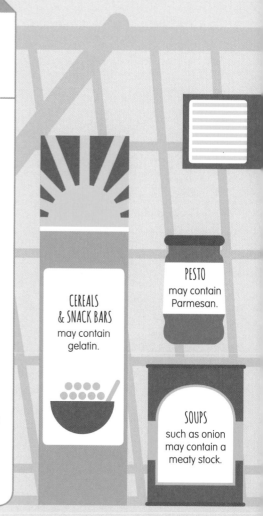

CEREALS & SNACK BARS may contain gelatin.

PESTO may contain Parmesan.

SOUPS such as onion may contain a meaty stock.

PRODUCTS TO WATCH OUT FOR

SOME FOODS appear vegan at first glance but actually contain hidden animal products. You can find vegan versions of many of these, but you can't assume! Below are a few key products to watch out for.

TIP
LOOK FOR TRUSTED VEGAN REGISTERED TRADEMARKS ON PRODUCTS TO GIVE YOU REASSURANCE.

MARSHMALLOWS & JELLY
products will usually contain gelatin.

RED & GREEN THAI CURRY PASTE
may contain fish sauce or dried shrimp.

BREADS
may contain milk powder or whey.

FRESH PASTA
contains egg—most dried doesn't, but it's best to check.

BREAD & DOUGH
products may contain L-Cysteine, an added amino acid that comes from duck feathers or hog hair.

SALAD DRESSING
may contain emulsifiers and egg yolk. Caesar dressing contains anchovies.

NOODLES
will often contain egg. Rice noodles, as well as some soba noodles, are a good choice.

MARGARINE
is not always vegan. It may contain whey, gelatin, or milk proteins.

CHIPS
may contain milk powder.

WINE & BEER
may have been refined using isinglass—check the label.

ORANGE JUICE
may have added lanolin-based vitamin D3.

WORCESTERSHIRE SAUCE
contains anchovies.

STOCKING YOUR VEGAN KITCHEN

Having a well-stocked vegan pantry and freezer really buys time and makes food prep easier, as so many plant-based items are nonperishable. Buy these ingredients regularly so you can whip up a meal at a moment's notice with the addition of some fresh produce.

NUTS AND SEEDS To keep these fresh, buy nuts and seeds in small quantities. Once open, keep in an airtight glass jar and away from sunlight. Whole nuts will keep much longer than shelled and ground. Pecans, peanuts, and walnuts will spoil the quickest, so keep in the refrigerator. Cashews and whole almonds will last the longest. Store seeds in jars in the refrigerator for ultimate freshness.

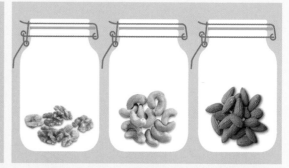

DRIED BEANS, PULSES, AND LENTILS With their long shelf life, these are invaluable for the vegan pantry. Once opened, keep in glass jars away of sunlight. Stock a mix of red, white, and black beans. Dried beans need soaking for 6-8 hours, so plan meals ahead. Lentils don't require soaking, making them the perfect convenience food. Also stock up on canned beans and cooked lentil pouches for ease.

GRAINS Whole grains are essential for the vegan diet; bulgur wheat, quinoa, farro, and pearl barley are all great examples. Store in glass jars away from sunlight.

RICE Store a selection of brown, white, basmati, red, wild, and arborio rice. A great vegan food to stock up on; when kept in a sealed container, rice will keep for years.

NOODLES AND PASTA You can store dried, egg-free versions of both noodles and pasta in your cupboard for 1-2 years. Choose whole-wheat pasta for higher fiber.

MAXIMIZING YOUR FREEZER

A GREAT WAY to save time and money is to batch cook meals for the freezer. This will make it much easier to maintain a new diet. Meals such as chilis, curries, and soups even get tastier as the flavors are left to mingle. Freezing key ingredients for vegan cooking is also a great time-saving trick. Below are the best foods to freeze.

WHOLE-WHEAT BREADCRUMBS	LASTS 3 MONTHS	Lots of vegan recipes need breadcrumbs for thickening or binding. Save all leftover bread and blend in a food processor in one batch. Seal in a container and freeze. These can be used from frozen.
CHICKPEAS AND BEANS	LASTS 1 YEAR	Having dried chickpeas or beans soaked, cooked, and frozen in portion sizes ahead is invaluable for the busy cook. You can then stir them right into dishes or run under warm water if wanting to blend.
AVOCADOS	LASTS 1 YEAR	It's good to stock avocados, especially if they are in danger of not being eaten in time. Peel, pit, and quarter, then open freeze on trays before putting into freezer bags. Remove and thaw before use.

NUTS AND FLOUR	LASTS 1 MONTH	Freezing will keep these fresher for longer, so they're a good option if you buy in bulk. Portion into plastic zipper-lock bags. Use them straight from the freezer. For ground nuts, pulse in a food processor first, then freeze.
HERBS AND SPICES	LASTS 1 YEAR	Buy difficult-to-find herbs and spices when you see them. These are great for adding exciting flavors to plant-based dishes. Freeze in small sealable bags and use straight from the freezer.
AQUAFABA	LASTS 1 MONTH	Thaw before use. Use to whip up meringues or use for cakes and baked goods as an egg replacement. Freeze in your required portion sizes or in ice cube trays, then transfer to a sealable freezer bag.

DAY 2

BREAKFAST
Berry & chia smoothie bowl
(pp.38-39)

LUNCH
Quesadillas with pinto beans & sweet potato
(pp.132-133)

DINNER
Vegetable stir-fry (pp.168-169)

SNACKS
Apple slices dipped into peanut butter,
Tropical immune boosters
(pp.62-63)

DAY 1

BREAKFAST
Superseed granola (pp.34-35)

LUNCH
Sweet potato, teff, & peanut soup (pp.100-101)

DINNER
Three-bean paella (pp.156-157)

SNACKS
Tropical immune boosters (pp.62-63),
Avocado & banana recovery
ice pops (pp.56-57)

DAY 3

BREAKFAST
Avocado, nori, & nut cream toast
(pp.36-37)

LUNCH
Creamy green soup
(pp.88-89)

DINNER
Rainbow lentil meatballs (pp.146-147)

SNACKS
Mung bean guacamole (pp.70-71),
Raw energy bars (pp.58-59)

DAY 4

BREAKFAST
Whole-wheat banana pecan
pancakes (p.51)

LUNCH
Vermicelli rice noodles (pp.142-143)

DINNER
Sweet potato and spinach curry (pp.162-163)

SNACKS
Carrot sticks and radishes with plant-based
yogurt, Raw energy bars (pp.58-59)

7-DAY MEAL PLAN

THIS IS A GREAT STARTING point
for new vegans. These simple
but tasty recipes will provide
variation and all the nutrients
you need over 1 week.

MEAL PLANNING

Planning your meals is a surefire way to make eating or cooking a plant-based diet much easier. A meal plan for the week is simple; you can stick to what you feel comfortable with at first and then get more creative as you become more confident. Having your food in the refrigerator and a recipe at the ready will also ensure you don't make bad food decisions when you are hungry. Meal planning ahead of time can also be an economical way of eating.

DAY 5

BREAKFAST
Almond milk oatmeal (pp.42-43)

LUNCH
Brown rice risotto with red peppers and artichokes (pp.160-161)

DINNER
Udon noodles with sweet and sour tofu (p.149)

SNACKS
Handful of almonds and dried apricots, Chickpea bites (p.66)

DAY 6

BREAKFAST
Lentil waffles (pp.32-33)

LUNCH
Seitan gyros (pp.126-127)

DINNER
Root vegetable stew (pp.108-109)

SNACKS
Lemony spinach hummus (pp.64-65), Chickpea bites (p.66)

DAY 7

BREAKFAST
Ancient grains oatmeal with pear (pp.48-49)

LUNCH
Brown rice sushi bowl (pp.174-175)

DINNER
Turkish stuffed eggplant (pp.204-205)

SNACKS
Garlicky onion crackers (pp.68-69) with Cashew ricotta (p.66)
Peanut butter & banana balls (pp.54-55)

BREAKFAST & BRUNCH

flex it

As a treat for nonvegan members of the household, serve the waffles topped with bacon and a drizzle of maple syrup.

LENTIL WAFFLES
with five-spice berry sauce

SERVES 4
PREP 15 MINS
COOK 15 MINS

1½ cups **raspberries**
1¼ cups **blackberries**
1 cup **blueberries**
¼ tsp **five-spice powder**
1 **cinnamon stick**
1¼ cups **unsweetened almond milk**
¼ cup **canola oil**
2 tsp **vanilla extract**
3 tbsp **agave nectar**
2 cups **whole-wheat flour**
1½ tsp **baking powder**
½ cup cooked **yellow or red lentils**

1 In a small saucepan, combine the raspberries, blackberries, blueberries, five-spice powder, and cinnamon stick. Cover and cook over low heat for 15 minutes, stirring regularly, until the berries break down into a thickened sauce. Add 2–3 tablespoons of water as needed.

2 Meanwhile, in a small bowl, whisk together the almond milk, canola oil, vanilla, and agave.

3 Preheat a waffle maker. In a large mixing bowl, combine the flour and baking powder. Incorporate the almond milk mixture into the flour mixture. Gently fold in the lentils.

4 When the waffle iron is hot, spray it with cooking spray. Add ½ cup batter to each section and cook, according to the manufacturer's instructions, to make 4 waffles in total.

5 Remove the cinnamon stick from the sauce. Serve the waffles and sauce immediately.

the good stuff

The benefits of including lentils in your diet are numerous—they are high in protein but low in calories, so they make a great healthy, filling breakfast food. They also contain high levels of soluble fiber to help lower cholesterol and reduce the risk of heart disease.

flex it

For nonvegans, a drizzle of honey and a serving of plain yogurt would work well with this healthy breakfast.

SUPERSEED GRANOLA
with nuts, dried fruit, & chia seeds

SERVES 12
PREP 15 MINS
COOK 30–35 MINS

2 tbsp **coconut oil**
⅓ cup **maple syrup**
¼ tsp **fine salt**
1 tsp **ground cinnamon**
3⅓ cups **rolled oats**
2 tbsp **pumpkin seeds**
3 tbsp **sunflower seeds**
¾ cup **sliced almonds**
⅔ cup **hazelnuts**, roughly
    chopped
⅔ cup **dried fruit**, such as
    cranberries, cherries, raisins, and
    pitted dates, roughly chopped
⅓ cup **toasted coconut chips**
1 tbsp **chia seeds**
1 tbsp **golden flaxseeds**

1 Preheat the oven to 325°F (160°C). If the coconut oil is solid, melt it in a small saucepan. Once melted, remove it from the heat and whisk in the maple syrup, salt, and cinnamon.

2 Mix the oats, pumpkin seeds, sunflower seeds, almonds, and hazelnuts together in a large bowl. Pour the maple syrup liquid over the dried mixture and toss it very well to combine.

3 Spread the granola mixture over 2 large baking sheets. Place in the center of the oven and bake for 30–40 minutes, turning every 10 minutes. Ensure that the granola is spread out, so that it browns evenly. The granola is ready when it is golden brown and crunchy.

4 Allow the granola to cool, then mix in the dried fruit, toasted coconut chips, chia seeds, and flaxseeds. Serve with dairy-free yogurt or dairy-free milk, as well as fresh fruit. You can store the granola in an airtight container for up to 2 weeks.

the good stuff

Nourishing oats provide slow-releasing energy and help reduce levels of cholesterol in the blood. Nuts and seeds provide healthy unsaturated fats and essential B vitamins.

flex it

A delicious alternative for nonvegans: swap the nut cream for any cream cheese as the base.

AVOCADO, NORI, & NUT CREAM TOAST
with sesame seeds & basil

SERVES 4
PREP 15 MINS

8 slices **quinoa superseed loaf**
1½ **avocados**, sliced
9 **cherry tomatoes**, sliced
3 tbsp **nori seaweed**, shredded
1 tbsp **sesame seeds**
a few sprigs of **basil**

NUT CREAM
¾ cup **Brazil nuts**
2 tbsp **lemon juice**
1 tbsp **olive oil**
salt and freshly ground
   black pepper

1 To make the nut cream, put the ingredients in a blender or food processor and blend until combined. You may need to stop the machine occasionally to scrape the mixture down with a spatula. Gradually add 2 tablespoons of hot water to achieve a thick, creamy consistency. Season with salt and pepper.

2 Toast the bread and spread with nut cream. Top with the avocados, cherry tomatoes, nori, sesame seeds, and basil.

VARIATION

Top the nut cream with finely sliced radish, sliced cornichons, and sliced apple. Garnish with finely chopped dill.

the good stuff

Nori is packed with vitamin C and micronutrients such as iodine, which is essential because the body can't make it by itself—it is needed for the production of the thyroid hormone.

BERRY & CHIA SMOOTHIE BOWL
with mango & mulberries

SERVES 2
PREP 10 MINS

½ cup **frozen raspberries**
⅔ cup **frozen blueberries**
1 cup **nut milk**, such as
   almond
½ cup ripe **banana**
⅓ cup **avocado**, sliced
2 tbsp **chia seeds**
2 tbsp **acai berry powder**
   (optional)

TOPPING
½ small **mango**, peeled and sliced
1 tbsp **sliced almonds**
3 tbsp **raspberries**
1 tbsp **pumpkin seeds**
1 tbsp **dried mulberries**

1 Put the smoothie ingredients in a high-speed blender or food processor and blend until smooth. Transfer to 2 bowls.

2 Lay the mango slices in a starburst pattern over half the surface, then arrange the almonds, raspberries, pumpkin seeds, and mulberries in stripes on the other half.

VARIATION

Try adding 1 cup (around 4½oz) of raw beets (skin on) to the blender along with some chopped fresh ginger—if your smoothie is too thick, dilute it by adding more nut milk or a little cold water.

the good stuff

A real power bowl for breakfast—the high potassium in bananas can protect you from workout muscle cramps, so this bowl is a good choice before any morning exercise!

TROPICAL FRUIT SMOOTHIE BOWL
with coconut flakes & cashews

SERVES 2
PREP 10 MINS

1 cup **frozen mango**
⅓ cup **frozen pineapple**
½ cup **papaya**
1 cup freshly squeezed **orange juice** (or store-bought)
2 tbsp **hemp seeds**
¼ tsp **ground turmeric**
1 tbsp **lucuma powder** (optional)

TOPPING
seeds of ½ **passion fruit**
½ **kiwi**, sliced
1 tbsp **coconut flakes**
1 small slice **papaya**,
    cut into chunks
1 tbsp **cashews**
1 tsp **goji berries**
1 small slice **watermelon**,
    cut into chunks

1 Put the smoothie ingredients in a high-speed blender or food processor and blend until smooth.

2 Pour into 2 bowls and arrange the toppings on the surface in stripes.

VARIATION

Try some other flavors that go with tropical fruits—add a handful of fresh mint and basil leaves to the blender, along with a squeeze of lime.

the good stuff

This is a great meal to start the day. Mango, pineapple, and papaya are loaded with vitamin C, which will boost your immune system. Turmeric has powerful anti-inflammatory properties.

flex it

An easy swap for nonvegans, this oatmeal would be just as tasty with dairy milk.

ALMOND MILK OATMEAL
with grapefruit & cocoa

SERVES 2
PREP 5 MINS
COOK 15 MINS

½ cup **rolled oats**
1 cup **almond milk**
1 **pink grapefruit**, peeled and segmented
¼ tsp **dairy-free cocoa powder**
1 tsp **pistachios**, chopped

1 Put the oats in a saucepan, then stir in the almond milk and 1 cup of water. Bring to a boil, then reduce the heat to a gentle simmer. Cook for 10–15 minutes, stirring occasionally, or until creamy.

2 Spoon the oatmeal into a serving bowl, add the grapefruit, and sprinkle over the cocoa powder and pistachios.

VARIATION

For a variation, top your oat meal with peach or apricot halves, a sprinkle of chopped almonds, and a drizzle of maple syrup.

the good stuff

Pistachios are full of antioxidants that help to shield the body from harmful chemicals—free radicals. Grapefruit packs a powerful nutritional punch, providing nearly half your daily vitamin C requirements.

QUINOA & BUCKWHEAT GRANOLA
with seeds & apricots

SERVES 4–6
PREP 10 MINS, plus soaking
COOK 55 MINS

1 cup **quinoa**
1¼ cups **rolled oats**
¾ cup **buckwheat groats**
⅔ cup **sunflower seeds**
⅔ cup **pumpkin seeds**
⅔ cup **chia seeds**
⅔ cup **shredded coconut**
¾ cup **walnut pieces**
1 tbsp **ground cinnamon**
½ cup **maple syrup**
¼ cup **coconut oil**
2 tsp **vanilla extract**
⅔ cup **raisins**
¼ cup **dried apricots**,
  finely chopped
nut milk, to serve

1 Preheat the oven to 325°F (160°C). Line 2–3 large baking sheets with parchment paper.

2 Put the quinoa in a sieve and rinse under cold running water. Put in a pan with 2 cups of water. Bring to a boil, cover, and simmer for 12 minutes or until al dente.

3 Strain and transfer to a mixing bowl. Add the oats, buckwheat, seeds, coconut, walnuts, and cinnamon.

4 In a small pan, gently heat the maple syrup, coconut oil, and vanilla until combined. Stir into the quinoa mixture and leave to soak for 10 minutes.

5 Spread out ½in (1cm) thick on the sheets. Bake for 20 minutes, then stir. Turn the oven down to 275°F (140°C) and bake for 20 minutes, then stir. Cook for 20 minutes more.

6 Combine the raisins and apricots and divide equally between the sheets. Leave to cool completely before serving or transferring to an airtight container.

the good stuff

The nuts, seeds, and grains in this granola are full of healthy fats and micronutrients. Dried apricots are rich in potassium, so adding them to your diet can help you maintain a healthy blood pressure.

flex it

A spoonful of plain yogurt would make a fabulous topping for nonvegans.

CHOCOLATE & HAZELNUT OATMEAL
with banana & maple syrup

SERVES 2
PREP 5 MINS,
 plus soaking
COOK 20 MINS

⅔ cup **rolled oats**

1⅓ cups **hazelnut milk**

⅓ cup **banana**, sliced

2 tbsp **maple syrup**

1 tbsp **raw cacao powder**

1 tbsp **hazelnuts**, crushed

TOPPING

1 tbsp **hazelnuts**, crushed

1 tbsp **cacao nibs**, crushed

½ **banana**, sliced

maple syrup, to taste (optional)

1 Put the oats, hazelnut milk, banana, maple syrup, cacao powder, and hazelnuts in a saucepan over medium heat. Bring to a boil, stirring all the time with a wooden spoon.

2 Lower the heat and simmer for 5 minutes, stirring often, until the oatmeal is the consistency you like. (Add more hazelnut milk, if you want it a little runnier.)

3 Transfer to bowls and serve immediately, sprinkled with the topping ingredients and drizzled with more maple syrup, if you'd like.

the good stuff

Oats are a good source of slow-releasing energy and are packed with iron. Cacao is a healthy "chocolate" option for vegans. It is supercharged with magnesium, calcium, iron, and zinc.

ANCIENT GRAINS OATMEAL WITH PEAR
topped with pistachio & pomegranate seeds

SERVES 1
PREP 10 MINS, plus soaking
COOK 15 MINS

1 tbsp **millet**

1 tbsp **amaranth**

1 tbsp **buckwheat groats**

1 tbsp **quinoa**

¾ cup **almond milk**, plus extra if desired

1 ripe **pear**, peeled and cored

1 tbsp **pomegranate seeds**

1 tbsp **pistachios**, crushed

1 tbsp **plant-based cream**, such as **coconut cream**

pinch of **ground cinnamon**

maple syrup, to taste

1 Combine the grains and soak overnight in double the volume of water. In the morning, drain and rinse well.

2 Place the grains in a saucepan with the almond milk. Bring to a boil, then turn down the heat and simmer gently for 15 minutes, stirring occasionally, until most of the almond milk is absorbed and the grains are soft—these grains have more texture and "bite" than oats.

3 Add some more almond milk if you like your oatmeal a little runnier.

4 Roughly mash half the pear with a fork and stir through the oatmeal. Cut the remaining pear into chunks.

5 Place the oatmeal in a bowl and top with the chunks of pear, pomegranate seeds, pistachios, a drizzle of the cream, and a pinch of cinnamon.

6 Sweeten with maple syrup to taste.

the good stuff

Pears contain plenty of fiber, so they are a good breakfast choice to help kick-start the digestive system. Pomegranate seeds contain high levels of antioxidants and vitamin B5, which helps you convert the food you eat into energy.

BREAKFAST BURRITOS
with mushrooms & black beans

SERVES 2
PREP 10 MINS
COOK 10 MINS

2 tbsp **olive oil**
½ small **red onion**, thinly sliced
2 cups **button mushrooms**, sliced
1 tsp crumbled **dried sage**
½ tsp **sea salt**
½ tsp freshly ground **black pepper**
⅓ cup cooked **black beans**
2 x 10in (25cm) **whole-wheat tortillas**
1 large **tomato**, diced
1 **avocado**, sliced
4 tbsp store-bought **salsa**

1 Heat the olive oil in a medium sauté pan over medium-high heat. Add the onion and mushrooms, and cook for 2–3 minutes, stirring once or twice.

2 Add the sage, sea salt, and black pepper, and cook for 2 more minutes.

3 Stir in the black beans and cook, turning a few times and pressing to break up the beans and brown them a little, for about 5 minutes. Remove from the heat and set aside.

4 Lay each tortilla on a plate. Spoon half of the mushroom filling down the center of each, then divide the tomato, avocado, and salsa between each burrito. Roll the burritos by folding two sides in first and then folding one long side inward.

the good stuff

Black beans make a healthy addition to a vegan diet, as they are high in protein with trace amounts of saturated fat and no cholesterol. They are also a great plant-based source of iron.

WHOLE-WHEAT BANANA PECAN PANCAKES
with fresh mixed berries

MAKES 12
PREP 15 MINS
COOK 10 MINS

1¼ cups **soy milk** or
   coconut milk, plus extra
   if needed
1 tbsp **ground flaxseeds**
1 tsp **apple cider vinegar**
1 large ripe **banana**, peeled and
   mashed well
1 tbsp **light brown sugar**
1 tbsp **maple syrup**, plus more for
   serving (optional)
1 tsp **vanilla extract**
1 cup **whole-wheat flour**
⅓ cup **buckwheat flour**
2 tsp **baking powder**
½ tsp **sea salt**
½ tsp **ground cinnamon**
¼ tsp **ground nutmeg**
⅔ cup **pecans**, toasted
   and finely chopped
⅔ cup mixed **raspberries**,
   blueberries, and/or **strawberries**
   (optional)

1 Warm ¼ cup of the soy or coconut milk in a small pan over medium-high heat.

2 Place the ground flaxseeds in a bowl, add the warmed milk, stir well, and set aside.

3 In a small bowl, whisk the apple cider vinegar into the remaining milk and set aside to thicken and curdle.

4 In another small bowl, mash the banana with the brown sugar, maple syrup, and vanilla. Whisk in the flax mixture, followed by the curdled milk, and blend well.

5 Heat a cast-iron grill pan or frying pan over medium heat until a drop of water sizzles and evaporates immediately.

6 Meanwhile, in a medium bowl, whisk together the whole-wheat flour, buckwheat flour, baking powder, sea salt, cinnamon, and nutmeg. Stir in the wet ingredients until just combined, and quickly fold in the chopped pecans. Stir in more milk, as needed, to make a thick batter; you want it to be the consistency of a heavy cake mixture.

7 Lightly oil or butter the grill pan, and drop 3 tablespoon-size scoops of batter into the pan, spreading with a small spatula if necessary. Cook for 2 minutes without disturbing or until bubbles form on the surface of the pancakes, carefully flip over the pancakes, and cook for another 1½ minutes. Grease the pan a little between each batch, as these pancakes may stick otherwise.

8 Serve hot with mixed fruit (if using) and more maple syrup (if using).

SNACKS & LIGHT BITES

flex it

Nonvegans can add a spoonful of honey into the mix to sweeten the energy balls and to help bind the ingredients.

PEANUT BUTTER & BANANA BALLS
with dates & hemp seeds

MAKES 16
PREP 20 MINS, plus chilling

½ cup unsalted **crunchy peanut butter**
1 small ripe **banana** (about ¼ cup)
1¾ cups **dates**
4 tbsp **ground flaxseeds**
3 tbsp **chia seeds**
¼ cup **ground almonds**
2 tsp **moringa powder**, to taste
shelled hemp seeds, to coat

1 Place all the ingredients except the hemp seeds in a food processor and pulse until the mixture starts to come together, forming a loose ball.

2 Divide into 16 evenly sized portions and roll into balls.

3 Sprinkle a layer of hemp seeds on a separate plate and gently roll the balls to coat.

4 Place in the refrigerator for 1 hour or in the freezer for 20 minutes to firm up before eating. Best served chilled.

the good stuff

A sugar-free peanut butter is a good energy source for a midmorning snack. These balls also contain moringa powder, a nutrient-dense leaf with a spinachy taste. Chia seeds are rich in fiber, omega-3 fats, protein, vitamins, and minerals.

AVOCADO & BANANA RECOVERY ICE POPS
with cacao & chia seeds

MAKES 8
PREP 10 MINS, plus chilling
COOK 5 MINS

1¾ cups **unsweetened almond** or **hazelnut milk**
2 tbsp **cacao nibs**
1 tbsp **chia seeds**
½ ripe **avocado**
1 small **banana**
pinch of **sea salt**

1 Pour the almond or hazelnut milk into a small pan and sprinkle in the cacao nibs. Warm gently, bring to a simmer, then remove from the heat. Leave to cool slightly, stir in the chia seeds, then leave to cool completely.

2 Place the avocado and banana into the bowl of a food processor and blend well with a pinch of sea salt. Add the cooled milk mixture to the bowl and blend again to break up the cacao nibs a little, but not so that they are smooth.

3 Using a small plastic funnel or a funnel made from parchment paper, pour the mixture into eight ¼-cup spherical ice pop molds. Alternatively, try ice pop molds or large ice cube trays. Place in the freezer.

4 When the pops are half-frozen, insert an ice pop stick or cake pop stick into each one. Return to the freezer and freeze until hard.

the good stuff

Avocados are loaded with good fats and are a good source of B vitamins. What's more, you are getting double the amount of potassium by eating avocado and banana. Adding a serving of chia seeds a day to your diet can help boost your metabolism.

flex it

Members of the household who eat dairy have the option of using sweet cocoa powder instead of cacao.

RAW ENERGY BARS
with dates & dried apricots

MAKES 16
PREP 20 MINS, plus chilling

1⅓ cups **Medjool dates**,
  pitted and roughly chopped
1 cup **dried apricots**,
  roughly chopped
½ cup **dried cherries** or
  cranberries, roughly chopped
⅔ cup **sliced almonds**
5 tbsp **cashews**,
  roughly chopped
¼ cup **pumpkin seeds**
¼ cup **sunflower seeds**
⅓ cup **coconut flakes**
2 tbsp **raw cacao powder**

1 Line a 8in (20cm) square baking sheet with parchment paper. Place the chopped dates in a heatproof bowl and cover with hot water. Leave them to soak while you prepare the rest of the ingredients.

2 After 5 minutes, drain the dates using a sieve. When cool enough to handle, press the dates lightly to remove some of the water, leaving them just a little damp. Place them in a food processor and add all the remaining ingredients.

3 Process the mixture until it is well combined, the nuts and seeds are in small pieces, and the mixture begins to form a ball in the bowl of the food processor. If the mixture is not blending thoroughly, take some out and process it in batches.

4 Dampen your hands and turn the mixture out onto the lined baking sheet. Push the mixture into an even layer using your hands. Dampen the back of a large metal spoon and use it to even out the mixture surface. Place the filled sheet in the refrigerator for 3–4 hours.

5 Turn the mixture out onto a board and cut into 16 squares. Wrap the squares individually in parchment paper to prevent them from sticking together, and store in an airtight container in the refrigerator until needed.

the good stuff

These no-bake bars combine fiber-rich dried fruit with protein-rich nuts and seeds. They are perfect to eat on the go as part of a plant-based diet, as they will provide tons of energy.

NUT & SEED NUTRIENT BOOSTERS
with chickpeas & lentils

MAKES 16
PREP 30 MINS, plus soaking
COOK 1 HR 20 MINS

⅓ cup **chickpeas**, soaked
   overnight
2½ tbsp **brown rice**
½ cup **red split lentils**
¾ cup **broccoli**, chopped
½ **red bell pepper**, seeded
   and finely chopped
1 **celery stick**, finely chopped
½ cup **pumpkin seeds**
¼ cup **sunflower seeds**
1 tsp **thyme leaves**
⅔ cup **cashews**
⅓ cup whole **almonds**
½ tsp **tamari**
1 tsp **brown miso paste**
sesame or **chia seeds**,
   to coat (optional)

1 Drain the soaked chickpeas and rinse under cold water. Place in a pan with 1¼ cups of boiling, salted water. Bring back to a boil, cover, and simmer for 1 hour until the chickpeas are soft but not soggy—they should have some "bite." Drain and put to one side.

2 Bring the brown rice to a boil in salted water, then simmer for about 30 minutes until really soft. Drain and put to one side.

3 Rinse the red lentils under cold water. Place in a pan with 1¼ cups of boiling, salted water. Bring back to a boil, cover, and simmer for 10 minutes until the lentils are soft but not soggy. Drain and put to one side.

4 Combine the rice, lentils, broccoli, red bell pepper, celery, pumpkin seeds, sunflower seeds, and thyme in a large bowl.

5 Put the chickpeas, cashews, almonds, tamari, and miso in a food processor and blend until you have a rough paste—you don't want a purée. Add this mixture to the rice bowl, combine well, and season.

6 Preheat the oven to 400°F (180°C). Line a large baking sheet with parchment paper. Divide the mixture into 16 evenly sized portions and roll into balls. If you wish, roll the balls in sesame seeds and/or chia seeds to coat them. Place on the baking sheet.

7 Bake in the preheated oven for 20 minutes until golden brown. Remove and leave to cool on a wire rack for a few minutes before serving hot. Alternatively, serve cold.

the good stuff

Due to the chickpeas and lentils, these powerful little bites are high in fiber and protein. This means they will boost your energy and keep you full for longer—curbing those unhealthy snack cravings. The nuts and seeds are packed with healthy fats and minerals.

TROPICAL IMMUNE BOOSTERS
with mango & goji berries

MAKES 16
PREP 20 MINS, plus chilling

1 cup **dried mango**
¼ cup **goji berries**
1 cup **cashews**
⅔ cup **unsweetened shredded coconut**, plus extra to coat
1 tbsp **baobab powder**
1¼ tsp **ground turmeric**
1 tsp **rosehip powder**
juice and zest of 1 **lime**

1 Place all the ingredients in a food processor and pulse until finely chopped.

2 With the motor running, add 2–4 tablespoons of cold water a little at a time until the mixture starts to come together, forming a loose ball.

3 Divide into 16 evenly sized portions and roll into balls.

4 Sprinkle a layer of unsweetened shredded coconut on a separate plate and gently roll the balls to coat.

5 Place in the refrigerator for 1 hour or freeze for 20 minutes to firm up before eating. Best served chilled, but fine popped in a lunchbox and eaten later in the day.

the good stuff

Turmeric is an anti-inflammatory; introducing it into the diet can help protect against colds and the flu. Goji berries pack a punch for their size—they are full of vitamins A and C, iron, potassium, and calcium.

LEMONY SPINACH HUMMUS
with tahini & chia seeds

SERVES 6
PREP 5 MINS

1 cup cooked **chickpeas**,
  peeled
⅓ cup **baby spinach**
2 **garlic cloves**
juice and zest of 1 large **lemon**
1 tbsp **tahini**
¼ cup **olive oil**
salt and freshly ground
  black pepper
1½ tbsp **chia seeds**,
  to garnish
alfalfa sprouts, to garnish
microgreens, to garnish

1 In a food processor, combine the chickpeas, spinach, garlic, lemon juice and zest, and tahini. Process on low for 1 minute to combine the ingredients.

2 With the processor on high, drizzle in the olive oil. For a thinner consistency, gradually add cold water 1 tablespoon at a time, until the desired texture is achieved. Salt and pepper to taste.

3 Transfer to a serving bowl and garnish with chia seeds, alfalfa sprouts, and microgreens. Serve immediately.

the good stuff

Leafy green spinach is a must for a vegan diet, as it is packed with vitamins K, A, C, B6, B12, and E. Vitamins C, E, and A are particularly good for your skin, cleansing it from the inside out.

flex it

For a meaty appetizer, top with 8oz (225g) sautéed minced lamb, spiced as desired.

CASHEW RICOTTA
with parsley & chives

SERVES 8
PREP 10 MINS, plus soaking

1¾ cups **cashews**

4 tbsp **extra virgin olive oil**

juice of 1½ **lemons**

2 tbsp **nutritional yeast**

1 tbsp finely chopped **parsley**

1 tbsp finely chopped **chives**

1 tsp **white (shiro) miso**

½ tsp **dried marjoram**

½ tsp **sea salt**

½ tsp freshly ground **black pepper**

1 Soak the cashews in water overnight.

2 Discard the soaking water, rinse the cashews well, and drain.

3 In a food processor fitted with a metal blade, process the cashews along with the olive oil, 4 tablespoons of warm water, the lemon juice, nutritional yeast, parsley, chives, miso, marjoram, sea salt, and black pepper until smooth.

4 Spread this nutty "cheese" on crackers, or use it as a filling for ravioli or lasagna. You can store it in the refrigerator for up to 5 days.

CHICKPEA BITES
with peanut butter

MAKES 24
PREP 15 MINS, plus chilling

¼ cup cooked **chickpeas**

½ cup **smooth peanut butter**

½ cup **rolled oats**

⅓ cup **agave nectar**

1 tsp **vanilla extract**

1 tsp **ground cinnamon**

pinch of **salt**

1 In a food processor, pulse the chickpeas until coarsely ground. Transfer to a large mixing bowl. Stir in the peanut butter, rolled oats, agave nectar, vanilla extract, cinnamon, and salt.

2 Take 1 heaped tablespoon of the chickpea mixture and roll into a ball with your hands. Repeat with the remaining chickpea mixture to make 24 in total. In an airtight container in the refrigerator, chill the bites for at least 1 hour, or overnight, to set before serving.

the good stuff

Chickpeas are packed with essential micronutrients. Oats are full of magnesium, which can help with moods. They also have a high fiber content, keeping you fuller for longer, which makes them the perfect snack food.

POLENTA FRIES
with rosemary & garlic

SERVES 4–6
PREP 15 MINS, plus chilling
COOK 30 MINS

1–2 tbsp **olive oil**,
   plus extra for greasing
2½ cups **vegetable stock**
1 tbsp **plant-based margarine**
1 cup **quick-cook polenta**
1 **garlic clove**, pressed
1 tbsp finely chopped **rosemary**
salt and freshly ground
   black pepper

1 Grease a baking sheet and set aside. Place the vegetable stock and margarine in a saucepan and bring to a boil. Then reduce the heat to medium-low and gradually add the polenta, whisking constantly. Cook for about 2 minutes, whisking constantly, until all the liquid has been absorbed and the polenta has thickened and is smooth.

2 Remove from the heat, add the garlic and rosemary, and mix well to combine. Transfer the polenta mixture to the baking sheet and spread it out to form an even ½in (1cm) thick layer. Place the baking sheet in the refrigerator to chill for 3 hours.

3 Preheat the oven to 400°F (200°C). Grease another baking sheet and set aside. Place the polenta on a clean surface and slice into long rectangular pieces. Spread out the fries on the prepared baking sheet and lightly brush with oil. Season well and bake for 20–25 minutes or until they are golden brown at the edges. Remove from the heat and serve immediately.

GARLICKY ONION CRACKERS
with a trio of seeds

MAKES 24
PREP 30 MINS
COOK 15 MINS

½ tbsp **sesame seeds**
½ tbsp **black sesame seeds**
½ tbsp **poppy seeds**
½ tsp **baking powder**
1¼ cups **chickpea flour**
¾ tsp **salt**
⅛ tsp **onion powder**
⅛ tsp **garlic powder**
2 tbsp **olive oil**

1 To make the topping, in a small bowl, combine the sesame seeds, black sesame seeds, and poppy seeds. Set aside.

2 Preheat the oven to 375°F (190°C). Prepare a clean, flat work surface and cut 2 large pieces of parchment paper, each about 12 x 16in (30 x 40cm).

3 To make the dough, in a large mixing bowl, combine the baking powder, chickpea flour, salt, onion powder, garlic powder, and olive oil. Gradually incorporate ¼ cup of water until a dough forms, adding additional water a spoonful at a time as needed, until the dough is just pliable. Place in the refrigerator to rest for 10 minutes.

4 Divide the dough into 2 pieces and place side by side between the two sheets of parchment paper, about 5in (12cm) apart. With a rolling pin, roll out as thinly as possible into 2 rectangles, about ⅛in (3mm) thick.

5 Remove the top sheet of parchment paper. With a pizza cutter or paring knife, score the dough into 1 x 1in (3 x 3cm) squares, making 24 crackers. Brush the dough with 1–2 teaspoons of water, then sprinkle the seed mixture evenly across the top.

6 Transfer the bottom piece of parchment paper directly onto a baking sheet. Bake for 10–15 minutes, until the edges start to brown and the crackers are firm. Leave to rest at room temperature for 5 minutes, then break the crackers apart. Store in an airtight container for up to 3 days.

MUNG BEAN GUACAMOLE
with lime & cilantro

SERVES 2
PREP 20 MINS

2 large **avocados**
juice of 1 **lime**
1 **onion**, finely chopped
2 **garlic cloves**, finely chopped
1 **tomato**, diced
½ cup cooked **mung beans**
2 tbsp roughly chopped
   cilantro leaves
salt and freshly ground
   black pepper

1 Cut the avocados in half, remove the pits, and scoop the flesh into a large bowl. Immediately add the lime juice. With a pastry cutter or fork, roughly mash the avocado.

2 Add the onion, garlic, tomato, mung beans, and cilantro. Stir gently to combine. Season with salt and pepper to taste. Serve immediately.

VARIATION

Swap the mung beans for black beans, or use a white bean such as cannellini beans. For a change, you could also stir through a few chopped green olives, red peppers, roasted garlic, or some toasted pumpkin seeds.

the good stuff

The addition of mung beans brings a nutritional boost and an extra creamy texture to this Mexican classic. Mung beans are an excellent source of folate, magnesium, and vitamin B1. They are also high in fiber and protein.

flex it

For a more substantial meal, nonvegans could top this dish with some finely sliced grilled steak.

CHICKPEA FLOUR SOCCA
with herb & green olive salad

SERVES 2
PREP 5 MINS, plus resting
COOK 15 MINS

1 cup **chickpea flour**
1 tsp **smoked paprika**
⅛ tsp **garlic powder**
pinch of **salt**
3 tbsp **olive oil**
2¼ cups **arugula leaves**
2 tbsp (10 sprigs) **flat-leaf parsley**
¼ cup (10 leaves) **basil leaves**
⅓ cup **green olives,**
  pitted and halved
juice of 1 **lemon**

1 To make the batter, in a medium mixing bowl, add the chickpea flour, smoked paprika, garlic powder, salt, 2 tablespoons of the olive oil, and 1 cup of water. Whisk to combine. Let rest at room temperature for 1 hour.

2 With the rack in the middle of the oven, place two 8in (20cm) cast-iron or heat-resistant frying pans in the oven and preheat to the highest setting. (The pans will heat up with the oven.)

3 When the frying pans are heated, carefully remove and swirl 1½ teaspoons of oil around in each. Pour half the batter into each and return to the oven. Bake for 8 minutes. Then broil/grill on a low setting and cook for an additional 2 minutes. Remove and let rest for 1–2 minutes.

4 Meanwhile, to make the herb and green olive salad, toss together the arugula, parsley, basil, green olives, and lemon juice. Place each socca on a serving plate and top with an equal amount of salad. Serve immediately.

the good stuff

Chickpea flour, also know as gram flour, is naturally gluten-free—it adds a nutty taste and a boost of protein. It's an excellent source of folate, necessary for supporting immune functions.

SPROUTED SUMMER ROLLS
with chile-lime dipping sauce

MAKES 8
PREP 20 MINS

¼ cup **bean thread** (glass)
  noodles
8 × 6in (15cm) diameter **rice**
  paper wrappers
1 **carrot**, peeled and julienned
  into 2in (5cm) pieces
1 × 2in (5cm) piece of **cucumber**,
  quartered, seeded, and
  julienned
handful of **radish sprouts**
handful of **mustard sprouts**
⅛ cup **pea shoots**
large handful of mixed **mint**,
  cilantro, and **Thai basil leaves**,
  roughly chopped

DIPPING SAUCE
½ mild **red chile**, finely chopped
½ **garlic clove**, very finely sliced
2 tbsp **rice wine vinegar**
1 tbsp **lime juice**
1 tbsp **granulated sugar**
1 tsp fine **sea salt**

1 To make the dipping sauce, whisk together the red chile, garlic, rice wine vinegar, lime juice, sugar, and sea salt with 3 tablespoons of warm water. Set aside.

2 To prepare the noodles, place in a bowl and cover with just-boiled water. Let sit for 5 minutes, then drain and dry well.

3 Soak 1 rice paper wrapper in a bowl of warm water for 10–15 seconds. Once soft, place the wrapper on a clean, damp kitchen towel. On the lower one-third of the paper, make a rectangular pile of 1 tablespoon of the noodles and equal quantities of the vegetables, sprouts, and shoots, leaving a ½in (1cm) border on each side. Top with a sprinkle of the herbs.

4 Lift the lower edge of the rice paper and fold it over the filling. Tightly tuck the sides in and over the edges of the filling, then roll up the summer roll, keeping the filling tucked in.

5 Place the roll seam-side down on a serving plate and cover with a second clean, damp kitchen towel. Continue to make the rolls until all the filling is used up. When you have made the last roll, serve immediately with the dipping sauce alongside.

the good stuff

Radish sprouts and mustard sprouts are super nutritious, as they are full of vitamin B6, a metabolism-boosting nutrient essential to include in a vegan diet. Raw sprouted seeds carry a risk of foodborne bacteria, so avoid serving to children and pregnant women.

flex it

To satisfy nonvegan members of the household, add cooked chopped shrimp or cooked crab meat to the roll filling in step 3.

ALMOND & BREADCRUMB STUFFED PEPPERS
with chiles & capers

SERVES 4
PREP 10 MINS
COOK 30 MINS

3 tbsp **extra virgin olive oil**
2 **garlic cloves**, finely chopped
1 small **shallot**, finely chopped
½ tsp crushed **chiles**
2 tbsp finely chopped
  flat-leaf parsley
½ cup fresh **breadcrumbs**
¾ cup **Marcona almonds**, finely
  chopped
1 tbsp **salted capers**, rinsed,
  drained, and finely chopped
1 × 14oz (400g) can whole **piquillo**
  peppers, drained

1. Preheat the oven to 350°F (180°C). Heat 1 tablespoon of the olive oil in a small saucepan over medium-high heat. Add the garlic, shallot, and crushed chiles, and cook for 30 seconds. Stir in the flat-leaf parsley and remove from the heat.

2. In a small bowl, combine the breadcrumbs, almonds, capers, and garlic mixture. Stir in 1 tablespoon of the olive oil.

3. Drizzle a medium baking dish with half of the remaining olive oil. Gently fill each piquillo pepper with about 1 tablespoon of the stuffing, and place the filled peppers in the baking dish. Drizzle the stuffed peppers with the remaining olive oil and bake for 20 minutes. Serve hot, warm, or at room temperature.

the good stuff

Garlic is not only an excellent source of B6, it also contains manganese, selenium, and vitamin C. Almonds are the healthiest of all the nuts and make a good ingredient to add to snack food. They are rich in vitamin E, calcium, and potassium.

ARANCINI (RISOTTO BALLS)
with panko breadcrumbs

SERVES 4
PREP 30 MINS, plus chilling
COOK 10 MINS

1 cup **all-purpose flour**
1½ cups **panko breadcrumbs**
about 2½ cups of your favorite
   leftover **risotto**, chilled overnight
10 x ½in (1cm) cubes **plant-based
   mozzarella cheese**
⅓ cup **frozen peas**
grapeseed oil, for frying
fresh **tomato sauce**, to serve

1 Line 2 baking sheets with parchment paper.

2 Place the flour, ½ cup of water, and breadcrumbs in separate small, shallow bowls.

3 Scoop out portions of about ¼ cup (about half a mug) of chilled risotto. Using wet hands, form each portion into a ball, tucking 1 plant-based mozzarella cheese cube and a few peas into the center. Place the balls on one of the baking sheets.

4 Working one at a time, quickly roll each ball in the flour, dip in water, and roll in the panko breadcrumbs, being sure to thoroughly coat each ball. Roll once more in the flour, shake off the excess, and set aside on the second baking sheet. When all balls are breaded, chill for 30 minutes or overnight.

5 Just before you're ready to serve, preheat the oven to 250°F (130°C).

6 Heat 3–4in (7.5–10cm) of grapeseed oil in a wide saucepan over medium-high heat. Use a deep-frying thermometer to bring the oil to 375°F (190°C) and add balls, 3 or 4 at a time. Cook, turning frequently, for about 3 minutes or until golden brown all over. Transfer to a wire rack set over a baking sheet to keep the balls crisp and keep warm in the oven as you fry subsequent batches. Serve hot with a fresh tomato sauce for dipping.

flex it

For a cheesy kick, nonvegans could stir some freshly grated Parmesan or pecorino into the mix.

flex it

Add raw ground lamb into the mix in step 3—the balls may require cooking for a little longer to ensure the meat is cooked.

BAKED FALAFEL
with pickled red onions & sambal oelek

MAKES 16
PREP 30 MINS, plus chilling
COOK 40 MINS

1 **garlic clove**
2 cups cooked **chickpeas**
½ tsp **baking soda**
½ tsp **ground coriander**
½ tsp **ground cumin**
pinch of crushed **dried chiles**
bunch of **curly parsley**, chopped
1¼ cups finely chopped **cilantro leaves**
juice and zest of 1 **lemon**
¼ cup **chickpea flour**
1 tbsp **olive oil**
salt and freshly ground **black pepper**
⅓ cup **sambal oelek**, to serve

PICKLED RED ONIONS
1 cup **apple cider vinegar**
½ cup **red wine vinegar**
2 tbsp **granulated sugar**
1 tsp **salt**
1 large **red onion**, thinly sliced

1 To make the pickled red onions, in a medium saucepan, bring the apple cider vinegar, red wine vinegar, sugar, and salt to a boil over medium heat. Stir until the sugar and salt dissolve. Remove from the heat and stir in the red onion. Leave to cool completely at room temperature, stirring occasionally. Pour into a glass jar and secure with a lid. Refrigerate for 3 hours or overnight.

2 Preheat the oven to 400°F (200°C). In a food processor, combine the garlic, chickpeas, baking soda, coriander, cumin, dried chiles, parsley, cilantro, and lemon zest and juice. Pulse until combined but not smooth.

3 Transfer the chickpea mixture to a medium mixing bowl and fold in the chickpea flour. Drizzle the olive oil over and stir once more until it holds together. Season with salt and pepper to taste.

4 Portion out approximately 2 tablespoons of chickpea mixture and roll into a ball with your hands. Place on a baking sheet and repeat with the remaining mixture. With a spatula, slightly flatten each one. Bake for 10 minutes, turn over, and bake for an additional 10 minutes. Serve immediately with the pickled red onions and sambal oelek on the side.

the good stuff

For a healthier version of falafel, these are baked instead of deep-fried. With chickpeas as the base, they are also full of protein and super filling.

SEITAN SATAY
with tamarind-peanut sauce

SERVES 4
PREP 5 MINS, plus chilling
COOK 10 MINS

10½oz (300g) **seitan**, cut into
   1in (2.5cm) chunks
6 tbsp **reduced-sodium tamari**
1 tbsp **toasted sesame oil**
1 tbsp melted **coconut oil**
3 tbsp grated **fresh ginger**
2 **garlic cloves**, finely
   chopped
8 **bamboo skewers**
2 tbsp **tamarind paste**
½ cup **crunchy peanut butter**
½ cup **full-fat coconut milk**,
   well shaken
1 tsp crushed **chiles**

1 Place the seitan chunks in a baking dish large enough to hold them in a single layer.

2 In a small bowl, whisk together 4 tablespoons of the tamari, 4 tablespoons of water, sesame oil, coconut oil, 1 tablespoon of the ginger, and garlic. Pour over the seitan, and stir well. Cover and refrigerate for 2 hours or overnight.

3 Soak 8 bamboo skewers in warm water for at least 30 minutes, then drain.

4 Preheat a grill pan and lightly brush it with oil.

5 In a medium bowl, whisk the tamarind paste with 2 tablespoons of hot (not boiling) water to soften. Add the peanut butter, coconut milk, remaining grated ginger, remaining tamari, and crushed chiles, and whisk well.

6 Thread the marinated seitan onto the skewers and cook, turning once or twice, for 5–7 minutes or until browned on all sides. Serve immediately with the tamarind-peanut sauce.

the good stuff

Seitan is a good protein choice for vegans—it's low in fat and contains high levels of vitamin B6. It's a good replacement for red meat.

flex it

The meat-eaters may prefer to skewer some lean chunks of steak and cook on the grill as per the recipe instructions.

THAI-STYLE FRITTERS
with bean sprouts & shredded vegetables

MAKES 8
PREP 20 MINS
COOK 25 MINS

½ **carrot**

¼ cup **asparagus spears**
(approx. 6in/15cm long)

½ small **red pepper**, seeded
and cut into thin strips

1 cup **all-purpose flour**

1 tsp **baking powder**

¼ tsp **ground turmeric**

¾ tsp **salt**

1 tsp grated **fresh ginger**

1 tsp finely chopped **lemongrass**
or **lemongrass purée**

1 **garlic clove**, crushed

1 thin **red chile**, seeded and
finely chopped

4 **scallions**, chopped

½ cup **bean sprouts**

1 tbsp chopped **cilantro**

sunflower oil, for frying

1 tbsp snipped **chives**, plus
extra to garnish

noodle and **bean sprout salad**
and **sweet chili sauce**, to serve

1 Pare the carrot into thin ribbons with a potato peeler or a mandolin. Cut the asparagus spears in half lengthwise and then widthwise. Set both aside with the red pepper.

2 Mix the flour with the baking powder, turmeric, salt, ginger, lemongrass, garlic, and chile. Whisk in 1 cup of cold water to form a batter the consistency of thick cream. Stir in the scallions, bean sprouts, and cilantro.

3 Place in 4 cooking rings in a large frying pan. Add about ¼in (5mm) sunflower oil and heat until hot but not smoking.

4 Add about an eighth of the batter (a small ladleful) to one of the cooking rings and quickly top with a few strips of each vegetable, pressing gently into the uncooked batter. Repeat with the other rings, using half the ingredients in all. Fry for 2–3 minutes until the batter is puffed up, set, and brown underneath.

5 Lift off the rings with tongs. Flip the fritters over with a spatula and fry for another 2 minutes to brown and cook the vegetables. Lift out with a spatula and drain, vegetable side up, on paper towels. Keep warm while cooking the remaining fritters in the same way.

6 Transfer the fritters to serving plates and garnish with a few snipped chives. Serve with a noodle and bean sprout salad and some sweet chili sauce for dipping.

SOUPS & STEWS

CREAMY GREEN SOUP
with wheat berries, leeks, & cannellini beans

SERVES 4
PREP 15 MINS
COOK 1 HR 20 MINS, plus cooling

2⅓ cups **wheat berries**
1 tbsp **light olive oil**
1 **onion**, finely chopped
2 **garlic cloves**, crushed
4 **leeks**, trimmed and
   finely sliced
1lb 2oz (500g) **spring greens**,
   stems removed and finely sliced
2½ cups **vegetable stock**
2 x 14oz (400g) cans **cannellini
   beans**, drained
salt and freshly ground
   black pepper

1 Put the wheat berries into a large heavy-bottomed saucepan and cover with cold water. Bring to a boil, then reduce to a simmer and cook, uncovered, for 45–50 minutes until tender but chewy. Drain them well and refresh under cold water before allowing them to cool.

2 Heat the olive oil in a large saucepan over medium heat. Add the onions and garlic and cook, stirring occasionally, for about 5 minutes.

3 Add the leeks to the pan and cook for about 10 minutes, stirring occasionally, until softened. Then add the spring greens and cook for another 2–3 minutes, or until they wilt.

4 Pour in the vegetable stock, bring to a boil, and allow the soup to simmer for about 10 minutes. Then add the cannellini beans to the pan and stir gently to mix. Transfer the soup to a food processor and pulse until it reaches a smooth consistency. Season to taste, if needed.

5 Return the soup to the pan and place over medium heat for 2–3 minutes to heat through. Then stir in the wheat berries and remove from the heat. Ladle into soup bowls, season with salt and pepper, and serve hot.

the good stuff

Wheat berries are the whole-grain form of wheat—full of fiber, low in calories, and good for digestion—making them the perfect addition to a plant-based diet. Leeks perk up this dish—full of vitamins K and A and magnesium, they keep your eyes and bones in good shape.

flex it

As a treat for nonvegans,
crispy cooked bacon would
make a lovely topping.

flex it

For nonvegans, stir in 5oz (140g) chopped, cooked, smoked turkey or ham when adding the stock and tomatoes.

HOPPIN' JOHN SOUP
with black beans & brown rice

SERVES 6
PREP 30 MINS
COOK 40 MINS

1 tbsp **olive oil**
1 small **onion**, diced
1 small **red bell pepper**, seeded
  and diced
2 **celery sticks**, diced
1 **garlic clove**, finely chopped
1 × 14oz (400g) can **chopped
  tomatoes**
2 sprigs of **thyme**
pinch of **ground cayenne pepper**
½ tsp **smoked paprika**
3½ cups **vegetable stock**
salt and freshly ground
  black pepper
1½ cups cooked **black-eyed peas**
1 cup cooked **brown rice**
½ cup chopped **scallions**
4 tsp chopped **flat-leaf parsley**

1 In a large saucepan, warm the olive oil over medium-low heat. Add the onion and cook for 2 minutes, or until it starts to become translucent. Add the red bell pepper and celery and cook for an additional 2 minutes. Add the garlic and cook for an additional minute.

2 Incorporate the tomatoes, thyme, cayenne pepper, paprika, and vegetable stock. Bring to a boil, then reduce the heat to low and cook, covered, for 20 minutes. Season with salt and pepper to taste.

3 Combine the black-eyed peas and brown rice. Cook for 10 minutes, or until the beans and rice are warmed through. Transfer to serving bowls and garnish with the scallions and parsley.

the good stuff

A combo of brown rice and black-eyed peas contains an impressive amount of fiber and will satisfy all your protein needs. Peppers and celery are thrown in for plenty of vitamins A and K.

CHUNKY BUTTERNUT SQUASH SOUP
with pearl barley

SERVES 4
PREP 10 MINS
COOK 50 MINS

½ cup **pearl barley**
2 tbsp **olive oil**
1 **onion**, diced
salt and freshly ground
 black pepper
2 **carrots**, sliced into thin rounds
1 **apple**, cored and diced
1 **red bell pepper**, seeded
 and diced
1 **butternut squash**, about
 2lb (900g), seeded and
 cut into cubes
3½ cups **vegetable stock**
1 tsp **ground cinnamon**
1 tsp **ground ginger**
1 tsp **sweet paprika**

1 Place the barley in a large saucepan, cover with 1½ cups of water, and bring to a boil. Reduce the heat to medium-low and cook for 25–30 minutes, or until tender. Then remove from the heat and drain any remaining water. Set aside.

2 Meanwhile, heat the olive oil in a large Dutch oven or saucepan over medium heat. Add the onions and season with a pinch of salt. Cook for about 8 minutes, stirring frequently, until they start to get translucent. Then add the carrots, apple, red bell pepper, and butternut squash. Stir to mix, and pour over the vegetable stock. Cover and cook, stirring occasionally, for about 30 minutes.

3 Add the cinnamon, ginger, and paprika. Cook for another 10 minutes. Remove from the heat and take out about ¾ cup of the vegetables with a slotted spoon and set aside. Use a hand-held blender to pulse the remaining mixture until it forms a smooth purée. Add the barley and reserved vegetables, season to taste, and mix well. Serve immediately.

the good stuff

Pearl barley is a versatile cereal with more fiber than other whole grains. Chewy in texture, it offers complex carbs and is rich in B vitamins, zinc, and magnesium. Butternut squash has key antioxidants and high levels of potassium.

INDIAN SPICED SOUP
with red lentils & kamut

SERVES 4–6
PREP 20 MINS
COOK 40 MINS

1 tbsp **light olive oil**

1 large **onion**, finely chopped

1 **leek**, trimmed and
finely chopped

1 × 2in (5cm) piece of **fresh ginger**,
finely chopped

2 tsp **mild curry powder**

4 **carrots**, unpeeled and
roughly chopped

1½ cups **red lentils**

1½ cups **kamut**

5½ cups hot **vegetable stock**,
plus extra if needed

salt and freshly ground
black pepper

1 Heat the olive oil in a large saucepan over medium heat. Add the onions and leeks and sauté for about 5 minutes. Then add the ginger and curry powder and stir to mix, adding a little water to the pan if they start to stick. Add the carrots, red lentils, and kamut to the pan and stir to mix.

2 Pour in 3½ cups of the stock, reserving the rest. Cover, reduce the heat to a simmer, and cook for 30 minutes or until the lentils have broken down, the kamut is tender, and the carrots are cooked through. Check the soup occasionally and add more stock as needed.

3 Remove from the heat and use a hand-held blender to process the soup until it reaches a chunky texture, adding more stock if necessary. Taste and season with salt and pepper. Stir well to combine and serve warm.

flex it

This is a great soup for using up roasted meat for a nonvegan treat. Slow-cooked lamb is really good—simply stir in some leftover meat just before serving.

MISO BROTH
with tofu & seaweed

SERVES 1
PREP 10 MINS, plus soaking
COOK 10 MINS

2 pieces of **dried
   wakame seaweed**
⅓ cup **spinach** leaves
⅛ cup **cabbage**, shredded
1 tbsp **brown rice miso**
1 × 2in (5cm) piece of **fresh
   ginger**, half grated, half finely
   sliced
1½oz (45g) **firm tofu**, chopped
   into cubes
sea salt and freshly ground
   black pepper
juice of 1 **lemon**
½ **scallion**, finely sliced
½ **red chile**, finely sliced

1 Place the wakame in a bowl and cover with hot water. Soak for 10 minutes, then drain and shred.

2 Meanwhile, steam the spinach and cabbage over boiling water for 3 minutes.

3 Pour 1 cup of boiling water into a saucepan, then stir in the miso paste with a fork for 2 minutes, or until it starts to dissolve. Bring to a boil, then reduce the heat to a gentle simmer and cook for 1 minute.

4 Add the grated ginger and tofu. Slowly pour in up to ½ cup of boiling water, tasting as you go and stopping when it tastes good to you. (Be careful not to dilute the miso too much.) Season with sea salt and pepper to taste, then simmer for 5 more minutes.

5 Add the spinach, cabbage, and wakame to a serving bowl, then ladle in the miso broth and tofu. Add a squeeze of lemon juice and sprinkle with the sliced ginger, scallion, and red chile.

the good stuff

Miso is a paste made from fermented soybeans. It is good to have in the pantry to whip up a healthy soup for vegans, and it also helps relieve fatigue. Dark green leafy seaweed is extremely good for you, containing high levels of calcium and increasing iodine levels.

flex it

For fish-eaters, add 7oz (200g) flaked white fish to the hot soup and simmer for a few minutes until cooked through.

flex it

Trout and beets are a flavor match made in heaven, so for fish-eaters, scatter over a handful of cooked flaked trout to serve.

BEET & BUCKWHEAT SOUP
with lemon yogurt sauce

SERVES 4
PREP 15 MINS
COOK 1 HR 5 MINS

1¼ cups **buckwheat**
1 tbsp **light olive oil**
1 **onion**, finely chopped
1lb 10oz (750g) **beets**, trimmed
  and cut into small chunks
2 cups **vegetable stock**
1 × 14oz (400g) can **chopped
  tomatoes**
salt and freshly ground
  black pepper
handful of **rosemary leaves**

LEMON YOGURT SAUCE
9oz (250g) **soy yogurt** or **coconut
  milk yogurt**
juice of 1 **lemon**

1 Rinse the buckwheat, then place in a medium saucepan and cover with 2 cups of boiling water. Cook for about 15 minutes until tender. Set aside.

2 Heat the olive oil in a large saucepan over medium heat. Add the onion and cook for about 5 minutes, stirring frequently, until translucent. Then add the beets and vegetable stock. Bring the mixture to a simmer and cook for 30–40 minutes, until the beets are tender.

3 Add the tomatoes to the pan and cook for 2–3 minutes. Transfer the soup to a food processor and pulse until it reaches a smooth consistency. Season to taste, if needed. Pour the soup back into the pan and heat through over low heat for 2–3 minutes. Remove from the heat.

4 For the sauce, place the ingredients in a bowl and stir to combine. Divide the soup among 4 bowls and top with the sauce. Then add equal quantities of the buckwheat, garnish with rosemary, and serve hot.

the good stuff

Reap the health benefits of adding beets to your plant-based diet, as they are packed with iron, which will reduce the risk of anemia. Beets also contain silica, an important component needed for the body to use calcium efficiently. Their natural sweetness is good for sating sugar cravings.

KABOCHA SQUASH SOUP
with lentils & ginger

SERVES 4
PREP 20 MINS
COOK 1 HR 40 MINS

1 **kabocha squash** (or **butternut squash**), seeded and cut into quarters

2 tbsp **olive oil**

1 **carrot**, chopped

1 **onion**, chopped

1 **celery stick**, chopped

4 cups **vegetable stock**

1¾ cups **yellow** or **red lentils**

2 tsp **curry powder**

½ tsp **ground ginger**

1 × 5.6fl oz (165ml) can **unsweetened coconut milk**

salt and freshly ground **black pepper**

1 **lime**, cut into 4 wedges

unsweetened toasted coconut flakes, to garnish

1 Preheat the oven to 350°F (180°C). Place the squash quarters cut-side up on a baking sheet and drizzle with 1 tablespoon of olive oil. Roast for 40 minutes, or until tender. Leave to cool.

2 Meanwhile, in a large saucepan, heat the remaining 1 tablespoon of oil over medium heat. Add the carrot, onion, and celery and cook for 3 minutes, or until translucent. Add 2½ cups of vegetable stock and the lentils and bring to a boil. Reduce to a simmer and cook, covered, for 45 minutes to 1 hour, until the lentils are tender. To ensure there is enough liquid for the lentils to absorb, add up to 1½ cups of additional stock as needed.

3 When the lentils are tender, scoop the roasted squash from its skin and add the flesh to the pan. Stir in the curry powder and ginger and heat through. With a blender or hand-held blender, purée until smooth. Stir in the coconut milk and heat thoroughly. Season with salt and pepper to taste. Serve with a lime wedge and some coconut flakes for scattering over.

the good stuff

Lentils are a nutritional powerhouse; they are full of protein and an excellent source of folate, the all-important B12 that must be included in a vegan diet.

flex it

For a meaty treat, fry 5½oz (150g) of cubed bacon lardons until cooked and golden, then scatter over the soup to serve.

SWEET POTATO, TEFF, & PEANUT SOUP
topped with coconut milk yogurt

SERVES 6–8
PREP 15 MINS
COOK 45 MINS

½ cup **teff**

1 tbsp **light olive oil**

1 **onion**, finely chopped

2 **garlic cloves**, finely chopped

1 tbsp **ground cumin**

1 × 14oz (400g) can **chopped
   tomatoes**

1lb 8oz (700g) **sweet potatoes**,
   unpeeled and cut into cubes

3½ cups **vegetable stock**

½ cup **smooth peanut butter**

salt and freshly ground
   black pepper

7oz (200g) **coconut milk yogurt**

6 tbsp roughly chopped **cilantro
   leaves**, to garnish

1 Place 1¾ cups of water in a large saucepan and bring to a boil. Add the teff and reduce the heat to a simmer. Cook for 10 minutes, stirring constantly, until all the water has been absorbed. Remove from the heat and set aside.

2 Meanwhile, heat the olive oil in a large saucepan over medium heat. Add the onions and garlic and sauté for about 5 minutes or until the onions have softened. Then add the cumin and sauté for another 2 minutes.

3 Add the tomatoes, sweet potatoes, and vegetable stock to the pan and reduce the heat to a simmer. Cover and cook for 30 minutes or until the potatoes are soft. Remove from the heat and use a hand-held blender to process the soup until smooth. Then add the peanut butter and process until fully incorporated.

4 Add the teff to the soup and stir through. Return the pan to medium heat and warm through for 2–3 minutes. Remove from the heat and season to taste, if needed. Ladle into soup bowls and top with a spoonful of yogurt. Sprinkle over the cilantro and serve hot.

the good stuff

Teff is a really good grain to include in a plant-based diet. It has high levels of vitamins and minerals and five times the iron found in wheat. This iron is also easily absorbed because teff contains low levels of phytic acid.

SUMMER PEA, MINT, & AVOCADO SOUP
with quinoa

SERVES 4
PREP 10 MINS
COOK 25 MINS

⅓ cup **quinoa**

2 **avocados**, pitted

1lb 2oz (500g) **frozen peas**

3 tbsp chopped **mint**, plus extra
  to garnish

3½ cups **unsweetened
  almond milk**

1 Rinse the quinoa under running water, drain, and place in a lidded
saucepan. Cover with 1⅛ cups of water and bring to a boil.

2 Reduce the heat to a simmer, cover, and cook for 15–20 minutes
or until almost all the liquid has been absorbed and the quinoa is
fluffy. Remove from the heat, drain any remaining water, and set aside
to cool.

3 Scoop out the flesh from the avocados and place in a food
processor. Add the peas, mint, and half the milk and pulse until
smooth. Then add the remaining milk and pulse until fully blended.

4 Divide the soup equally among 4 soup bowls. Top with equal
quantities of the cooled quinoa. Garnish with some mint and
serve immediately.

the good stuff

Peas offer a super serving of vitamin K. With
relatively high levels of protein, they also fill up
and satisfy you, so you're not left feeling hungry.

MEATY MUSHROOM STEW
with red wine & balsamic vinegar

SERVES 6
PREP 15 MINS
COOK 30 MINS

4 tbsp **extra virgin olive oil**

2 **onions**, finely chopped

1 small **shallot**, halved and
finely chopped

2 **celery sticks**, finely chopped

1 large **carrot**, finely chopped

4 cups tiny white **button
mushrooms**, halved

3 cups **hen of the woods
mushrooms**, sliced

3 cups **chanterelle mushrooms**,
sliced

3 **garlic cloves**, finely chopped

1 tsp **sea salt**, plus extra to taste

½ tsp freshly ground **black pepper**,
plus more to taste

1 tbsp **sweet Hungarian paprika**

1 tsp **dried thyme**

1 tsp **dried dill**

2 tbsp **all-purpose flour**

3–4 cups **vegetable** or **mushroom
stock**

1 cup **dry red wine**

1 medium **potato**, peeled
and diced

4 tbsp finely chopped **flat-leaf
parsley**

1 tbsp **balsamic vinegar**

1 Heat 2 tablespoons of olive oil in a 14-cup large, deep-sided pan over medium-high heat. Add the onions and shallot, and cook, stirring frequently, for 5 minutes.

2 Add the celery, carrot, all the mushrooms, and garlic, and cook, stirring frequently, for about 10 minutes or until the mushrooms begin to turn golden. Add the remaining olive oil as the mushrooms start to stick to the pan.

3 Stir in the sea salt, black pepper, sweet Hungarian paprika, thyme, and dill. Add the flour to the mushroom mixture and stir for 2 minutes.

4 Add 3 cups of vegetable or mushroom stock, red wine, and potato, and bring to a boil. Reduce the heat to medium and cook, stirring often, for 10 minutes or until the stew is thickened and vegetables are tender. Add additional stock if the stew is too thick for your liking.

5 Remove from the heat and stir in the flat-leaf parsley and balsamic vinegar. Taste, add more sea salt and black pepper if needed, and serve. The stew will keep in the refrigerator for up to 5 days and is even more delicious the next day.

the good stuff

Mushrooms contain healing benefits, including antimicrobial and antibacterial properties. They are also packed with vitamins C and D; potassium; and several beneficial minerals that may be harder to get in a plant-based diet, such as selenium, copper, iron, phosphorus, and potassium.

SUMMER BEAN STEW
with wheat berries

SERVES 4
PREP 20 MINS, plus soaking
COOK 55 MINS

¾ cup **wheat berries**
1 tbsp **light olive oil**
1 **onion**, finely chopped
2 **garlic cloves**,
   finely chopped
2 **celery sticks**,
   finely chopped
2 **yellow** or **red bell peppers**,
   seeded and diced
1 **zucchini**, diced
2 cups **vegetable stock**
1 × 14oz (400g) can **navy beans**,
   drained
1 × 14oz (400g) can **borlotti beans**,
   drained
1 × 14oz (400g) can **chopped
   tomatoes**
2 tsp **Italian herb seasoning**
salt and freshly ground
   black pepper
handful of **basil leaves**,
   to garnish

1 Place the wheat berries in a large bowl and cover with water. Leave to soak overnight or for at least 8 hours. Then drain any remaining water and rinse under running water. Drain well and set aside.

2 Heat the olive oil in a large soup pot over medium heat. Add the onions and garlic and sauté for about 3 minutes or until the onions are translucent. Add the celery and sauté for another 2 minutes. Then add the bell peppers and zucchini and cook for 3 minutes, stirring frequently.

3 Add the vegetable stock, wheat berries, navy beans, borlotti beans, tomatoes, and Italian seasoning. Stir well and reduce the heat to a simmer. Cover and cook for 45 minutes, until the vegetables and wheat berries are tender. Season to taste, if needed, and remove from the heat. Serve hot, garnished with basil.

the good stuff

This bowl of stew will provide you your daily quota of fiber, thanks to the multitasking beans, which are also part of a balanced diet.

flex it

This stew is delicious on its own but could be served with some grilled lamb chops for meat-eaters.

ROOT VEGETABLE STEW
with sprouted barley & sorghum

SERVES 4
PREP 10 MINS
COOK 1 HR 10 MINS

4 tbsp **olive oil**
2⅓ cups **young turnips**, chopped
2⅓ cups **carrots**, chopped
2¼ cups **parsnips**, chopped
1 **onion**, finely chopped
2 **celery sticks**, peeled and
   finely chopped
½ cup **sprouted barley**
1 cup **sorghum grains**
7 cups **vegetable stock**
1 tsp chopped **thyme leaves**
salt and freshly ground
   black pepper
2½ tbsp finely chopped
   flat-leaf parsley

1 In a casserole dish or large, heavy-based saucepan with a lid, heat the olive oil over medium heat. Add the turnips, carrots, and parsnips and cook for 5 minutes, turning occasionally, until they begin to brown. Remove them from the pan and set aside.

2 Add the onion and celery to the pan and cook over medium heat for 3 minutes until they start to soften but do not brown. Add the barley and sorghum and cook for another 2 minutes until the grains start to color.

3 Add the vegetable stock and thyme, and season well with salt and pepper. Bring to a boil, then reduce the heat to a simmer, cover, and cook for 40 minutes; the grains will be partially cooked.

4 Remove the lid and increase the heat. Add the browned root vegetables and parsley and return to a boil. Reduce the heat to a simmer and cook, uncovered, for a final 20 minutes until the vegetables have softened and the stock has reduced. Season with salt and pepper, if needed, and serve immediately.

the good stuff

As well as its robust flavor, barley is a good source of micronutrients—sprouted grains activate enzymes, improve amino acids, have a high vitamin content, and are easier to digest.

POSOLE (MEXICAN VEGETABLE STEW)
mushrooms & hominy

SERVES 4–6
PREP 10 MINS
COOK 20 MINS

3 tbsp **olive oil**

1 large **onion**, finely chopped

2 **carrots**, cut into ½in
(5mm) rounds

3 cups **chestnut mushrooms**,
thinly sliced

2 **garlic cloves**, finely chopped

3 tbsp **dried ground New Mexico
chili powder**

1 tsp **ground cumin**

1 tsp **sea salt**

½ tsp **dried oregano**

3½ cups **vegetable stock**

2½ cups **hominy** or **sweetcorn**,
rinsed and drained

1 **zucchini**, trimmed, quartered
lengthwise, and cut into ½in
(1cm) chunks

juice of 1 **lime**

2 tbsp finely chopped
cilantro leaves

1 Heat the olive oil in a large, deep-sided pan or stockpot over medium-high heat. Add the onion and cook, stirring frequently and adjusting the heat as necessary, for 5 minutes.

2 Stir in the carrots and mushrooms, and cook for 5 minutes.

3 Add the garlic and stir for 1 minute.

4 Sprinkle the chili powder, cumin, sea salt, and oregano over the vegetable mixture and stir for 30 seconds.

5 Add the vegetable stock, bring to a simmer, and cook for 5 minutes.

6 Add the hominy or sweetcorn and zucchini, bring to a boil, reduce the heat to medium-low, and cook for 10 minutes.

7 Remove from the heat, stir in the lime juice and cilantro, and serve.

the good stuff

Get multiple servings of veggies in this tasty pot. Carrots are a low-calorie food stacked with vitamin A, which helps keep your vision at its best.

flex it

Fry 7oz (200g) raw, smoked sausage until golden and cooked and top the soup with it for the meat-eaters.

PINTO BEAN PEANUT STEW
with sweet potatoes & greens

SERVES 6
PREP 25 MINS
COOK 45 MINS

1 tbsp **coconut oil**
1 small **onion**, chopped
1 **garlic clove**, finely chopped
1 large **sweet potato**, peeled and
   cut into 1in (3cm) cubes
1 tsp **ancho chili powder**
½ tsp **cayenne pepper**
2¼ cups **chopped tomatoes**
2 cups **vegetable stock**
½ cup **smooth peanut butter**
2½ cups cooked **pinto beans**
1 cup chopped **leafy greens**
salt and freshly ground
   black pepper
chopped **cilantro leaves**,
   to garnish

1 In a medium stockpot, heat the coconut oil over medium-low heat until shimmering. Add the onion and cook for 2–3 minutes until soft. Add the garlic and cook for 1 minute.

2 Add the sweet potato, ancho chili powder, and cayenne pepper. Stir to combine. Pour in the tomatoes and vegetable stock. Bring to a boil, then reduce to a simmer and cook, uncovered, for 5 minutes.

3 Stir in the peanut butter. Return to a boil, then reduce the heat and simmer, covered, for 10 minutes.

4 Fold in the pinto beans and greens. Return to a boil once more, then reduce to a simmer and cook, covered, for 15 minutes, or until the greens are tender. Season with salt and pepper to taste. Garnish with the cilantro and serve immediately.

the good stuff

Canned tomatoes, full of carotenoids, are a wonder staple for the pantry. There are also plenty of dark leafy greens in this, which are rich in minerals, particularly iron.

BURGERS, SANDWICHES, & WRAPS

AMARANTH BLACK BEAN BURGERS
with avocado cream

MAKES 6
PREP 15 MINS, plus cooling
COOK 45 MINS

⅓ cup **amaranth**

1 × 14oz (400g) can **black beans**,
   drained

1 small **red onion**, finely chopped

½ tsp **garlic granules**
   or ¼ tsp **garlic powder**

½ tsp **chili flakes**

2 tbsp **rolled oats**

¼ tsp **salt**

6 **burger buns**, to serve

handful of **cherry tomatoes**,
   thinly sliced, to serve

1 small **red onion**, sliced
   into rings, to serve

AVOCADO CREAM

2 **avocados**

juice of 1 **lemon**

pinch of **salt**

1 Place the amaranth in a large saucepan and cover with ½ cup of water. Bring to a boil, then reduce to a simmer, and cook for 12 minutes or until all the water has been absorbed. Remove from the heat, drain any remaining water, and leave to cool slightly.

2 Preheat the oven to 400°F (200°C). Grease and line a baking sheet with parchment paper. Transfer the amaranth to a large bowl. Add the black beans, red onion, garlic, and chili flakes. Mix well, using the back of a fork to mash the ingredients together. Then add the rolled oats and salt to the mixture. Mix until well incorporated.

3 Divide the mixture into 6 equal portions and shape into balls. Gently press down each ball to form a burger patty about 3in (7.5cm) in diameter. Place the burgers on the prepared baking sheet and transfer to the oven. Bake for 30 minutes or until they are firm to the touch and crispy on the outside.

4 For the avocado cream, scoop out the flesh from the avocado and place in a food processor. Add the lemon juice and salt and pulse until smooth. Place the burgers in the buns and top with the avocado cream. Serve with the cherry tomatoes and red onions.

the good stuff

Amaranth contains plenty of protein and all the amino acids your body needs. It is also a good source of calcium and has high levels of zinc.

KOREAN BARBECUE SLIDERS
with tempeh & lettuce

MAKES 8
PREP 15 MINS, plus marinating
COOK 20 MINS

1⅓ cups **tempeh**
½ cup plus 1 tsp **low-sodium tamari**
¼ cup **light brown sugar**
3 **garlic cloves**, finely chopped
1 tbsp **sambal oelek**
1 tbsp finely chopped **fresh ginger**
1 tbsp plus 2 tsp **rice vinegar**
2 tsp **toasted sesame oil**
1 tbsp **cornstarch**
1 tsp **toasted sesame seeds**
1 tsp **granulated sugar**
8 **small buns**, such as **whole-wheat rolls** or **slider buns**
1 cup **romaine lettuce**, shredded
½ cup **radishes**, thinly sliced

1 Place the tempeh in a small frying pan, cover with water, set over medium heat, and bring to a simmer. Cover and cook for 10 minutes. Remove the lid, drain, and cool. Cut into 2 horizontal slices, then cut each into 4 equal pieces, so you have 8 small "burgers." Place the tempeh slices in a shallow pan that will accommodate them in a single layer.

2 In a small pan over high heat, combine ½ cup of the tamari, brown sugar, garlic, sambal oelek, ginger, 1 tablespoon of the rice vinegar, and 1 teaspoon of the sesame oil. Bring to a boil.

3 In a small bowl, combine the cornstarch and 1 tablespoon of water until smooth. Add to the sauce and cook for 1 minute or until thickened.

4 Pour the hot barbecue sauce over the tempeh and marinate at room temperature for 30 minutes (or up to 24 hours in the fridge).

5 Preheat a grill to high. In a bowl, whisk together the 2 teaspoons of rice vinegar, remaining 1 teaspoon of tamari, remaining 1 teaspoon of sesame oil, toasted sesame seeds, and granulated sugar. Set aside.

6 Grill the tempeh slices, turning once, until they're hot and crispy. Place 1 tempeh slice on each bun.

7 In a small bowl, toss the romaine lettuce and radishes with the dressing. Distribute among the buns and serve immediately.

the good stuff

Tempeh is high in protein and also rich in minerals, copper, and manganese—which helps to clear glutamate, a nerve toxin, from your brain.

BÁNH MÌ PORTOBELLO BURGERS
with pickled vegetables

SERVES 4
PREP 40 MINS
COOK 10 MINS

4 large **portobello mushrooms**,
 stems removed
2 tbsp **plant-based mayonnaise**
1 tsp **Sriracha hot sauce**
4 x 4in (10cm) pieces crusty
 baguette, split
½ **cucumber**, thinly sliced
cilantro leaves (optional)

MARINADE
juice of 1 **lime**
2 tbsp **low-sodium tamari**
 or **soy sauce**
1 tsp **toasted sesame oil**
½ tsp **garlic powder**
½ tsp **ground ginger**

PICKLED VEGETABLES
1 small **daikon radish**, peeled
 and shredded
1 **carrot**, shredded
4 tbsp **rice vinegar**
1 tbsp **granulated sugar**
1 tsp **sea salt**

1 In a small bowl, whisk together the marinade ingredients. Wipe each mushroom clean with damp paper towel, place mushrooms in a zipper-lock plastic bag, pour in the marinade, seal the bag, and shake gently to distribute the marinade. Set aside.

2 To make the pickled vegetables, gently toss the daikon radish and carrot in a medium bowl. In a small saucepan over medium heat, combine the rice vinegar, sugar, and sea salt with 4 tablespoons of water. Bring to a boil, stirring to dissolve the sugar and salt. Pour the vinegar mixture over the daikon and carrot, and stir. Set aside for about 30 minutes, then drain.

3 In another small bowl, whisk together the plant-based mayonnaise and the Sriracha hot sauce.

4 Preheat a grill to high or set a grill pan over high heat on your stove. Place the mushrooms on the grill, gill side down, and cook for 3 minutes. Turn them over and cook for another 2 minutes or until the mushrooms are juicy and tender. During the last minute of mushroom cooking time, place the baguette pieces on the grill, split side down, to toast.

5 To assemble the sandwiches, spread one-quarter of the mayonnaise mixture on one side of each baguette and add a layer of cucumber slices. Place 1 mushroom burger on each sandwich and top with one-quarter of the drained pickled vegetables. Garnish with cilantro leaves (if using), and serve immediately.

PUY LENTIL & MUSHROOM BURGERS
with lettuce, tomato, & onion

MAKES 4
PREP 15 MINS, plus chilling
COOK 40–45 MINS

½ cup **Puy lentils**
3 tbsp **olive oil**, plus extra
  for frying the burgers
1 **onion**, finely chopped
1lb (450g) **portobello mushrooms**,
  cleaned, trimmed, and
  roughly chopped
2 **garlic cloves**, crushed
1 tsp **thyme leaves**, chopped
1 tbsp finely chopped
  flat-leaf parsley
1 tbsp **balsamic vinegar**
1⅓ cups **fresh white breadcrumbs**
1 tbsp **nutritional yeast**
salt and freshly ground
  black pepper
whole-wheat buns, **lettuce leaves**,
  tomato slices, and **red onion**
  slices, to serve

1 Place the lentils in a saucepan of cold water and bring to a boil. Reduce to a low simmer, skimming off any foam from the top, and cook for 15 minutes until just soft. Drain and rinse, then leave to cool.

2 Heat 1 tablespoon of the olive oil in a large, nonstick frying pan. Cook the onion over medium heat for 5 minutes, until softened but not brown. Add the remaining oil and the portobello mushrooms, and cook for another 15–20 minutes, until they break down and there is no moisture left in the pan. Add the garlic, thyme, and parsley and cook for another minute, until the garlic is fragrant. Add the balsamic vinegar and remove from the heat.

3 Put the mushroom mixture, cooled lentils, breadcrumbs, and nutritional yeast into a food processor and season well. Pulse carefully until it is just mixed and still has some texture.

4 Allow the mixture to cool for 5 minutes. Shape the cooled mixture into 4 equal-sized patties and chill, covered, for 30 minutes to allow them to firm up.

5 Clean the frying pan with a piece of paper towel. Heat a little oil in the pan and cook the burgers over medium heat for 3–4 minutes on each side, until well browned and cooked through. Serve in whole-wheat buns, with your choice of accompaniments.

the good stuff

Protein-packed Puy lentils are rich in soluble fiber, which stabilizes your blood sugar and makes you feel full for longer. Onions are surprisingly high in vitamin C and full of probiotic fiber.

FALAFEL BURGERS
with tahini & garlic dressing

SERVES 4
PREP 15 MINS
COOK 10 MINS

1 tbsp **ground flaxseeds**

4 or 5 tbsp **warm water**

4 tbsp **extra virgin olive oil**

1 **onion**, finely chopped

2 tsp **ground cumin**

1 tsp **ground coriander**

½ tsp **sea salt**

½ tsp freshly ground **black pepper**

1 tsp **lemon** zest

juice of 2 **lemons**

4 tbsp finely chopped **cilantro leaves**

2 tbsp finely chopped **flat-leaf parsley**

2 x 14oz (400g) cans **chickpeas**, drained and rinsed, 4 tbsp liquid reserved

1⅓ cups **fresh breadcrumbs**

3 tbsp **grapeseed oil**

2 tbsp **tahini**

1 **garlic clove**, minced

4 **pita breads**, split on one side

2 **plum tomatoes**, finely diced

½ cup **romaine lettuce**, thinly sliced

½ **red onion**, thinly sliced

1 In a small bowl, combine the flaxseeds and 3 tablespoons of warm water. Set aside.

2 Heat 2 tablespoons of the olive oil in a small frying pan over medium heat, until it shimmers (but before it begins to smoke). Add the onion, cumin, and coriander, and sauté, stirring constantly, for 5 minutes or until the onion softens and begins to brown.

3 Stir in the sea salt, black pepper, lemon zest, and 2 tablespoons of lemon juice. Remove from the heat, and stir in the cilantro and flat-leaf parsley.

4 In a food processor fitted with a metal blade, process the chickpeas, breadcrumbs, and onion mixture for 1 minute or until chunky. Reserve 4 tablespoons of the mixture. Continue to process, adding the flax mixture, the remaining olive oil, and the reserved liquid from the chickpeas, until smooth. Pulse in the reserved chickpea mixture in 1 or 2 pulses, to evenly distribute. Divide the mixture into 8 evenly sized burgers 3in (7.5cm) wide and about 1in (2.5cm) thick.

5 In a large nonstick frying pan over medium-high heat, heat the grapeseed oil. Add the falafel "burgers" and cook, turning once, until both sides are golden brown and the falafels are heated through.

6 In a small bowl, whisk together the tahini, garlic, and remaining lemon juice. Add 1 or 2 tablespoons of warm water, or enough to make a smooth dressing.

7 Fill each pita with 2 falafel burgers and evenly divide the plum tomatoes, romaine lettuce, and red onion between the pitas. Drizzle the pitas with the tahini mixture, and serve immediately.

PAN BAGNAT
with artichokes & capers

MAKES 4
PREP 20 MINS

1 x 14oz (400g) can **chickpeas**,
  rinsed and drained
1 x 6oz (170g) jar marinated grilled
  artichoke hearts, drained,
  2 tbsp marinade reserved
1 tbsp **salted capers**, rinsed
  and drained
1 tbsp **red wine vinegar**
1 tsp **dulse flakes**
4 crusty round **whole-wheat
  rolls**, sliced
2 large **tomatoes**, sliced
4 leaves **romaine lettuce**
½ small **red onion**, sliced
  paper thin
2 tbsp chopped, pitted
  black olives
4 tbsp **extra virgin olive oil**
½ tsp freshly ground **black pepper**

1 In a food processor fitted with a metal blade, pulse the chickpeas, artichoke hearts, reserved artichoke heart marinade, capers, red wine vinegar, and dulse flakes until a rough, chunky purée consistency is reached.

2 Divide the chickpea mixture equally among the rolls. Top with tomato slices, romaine lettuce, and red onion slices.

3 Sprinkle the black olives over the vegetables, drizzle each sandwich with 1 tablespoon of olive oil, and season liberally with black pepper. Serve with plenty of napkins!

VARIATION

For a variation, top the bread with wild arugula leaves, grilled eggplant slices, and finely sliced red onion. Then scatter over chopped green olives, and finish with a drizzle of chili oil.

the good stuff

Dulse is a good source of potassium and iron and is rich in iodine and vitamin B6; it is invaluable for a plant-based diet.

flex it

Nonvegans can use ordinary tzatziki here instead, and perhaps add a slice of Havarti or Cheddar cheese to the wrap, too.

SEITAN GYROS
with plant-based tzatziki

MAKES 6
PREP 30 MINS
COOK 10 MINS

4 tbsp **extra virgin olive oil**,
  plus extra for grilling
juice of 2 **lemons**
2 tbsp finely chopped **flat-leaf
  parsley**
1 tsp **sea salt**
½ tsp freshly ground **black pepper**
1 **garlic clove**, crushed and
  finely chopped
1 loaf **seitan**
6 **pita breads** (vegan)
3 cups shredded **romaine
  lettuce**
3 **plum tomatoes**, cored
  and cut into small dice
½ small **red onion**, very
  thinly sliced
plant-based tzatziki or 1 cup
  plant-based yogurt mixed with
  juice of ½ **lemon**
1 tsp **sweet paprika**

1 In a small bowl, whisk together the olive oil, lemon juice, flat-leaf parsley, sea salt, black pepper, and garlic.

2 Slice the seitan loaf very thinly and place the slices in a single layer on a large baking dish. Pour the marinade over the top and set aside at room temperature for 25 minutes.

3 Preheat a grill and brush the grill with a little olive oil.

4 Remove the seitan slices from the marinade, add to the grill, and grill for about 1 minute per side or until charred.

5 Quickly grill the pita breads just to warm them. Evenly divide the seitan among the pita, and top with romaine lettuce, plum tomatoes, and red onion. Drizzle each gyro with the plant-based tzatziki, sprinkle with sweet paprika, roll up, and serve immediately.

the good stuff

Seitan is a high-protein, low-calorie food, as well as cholesterol-free and non-GMO. You can get your daily amount of riboflavin (B2) and B3 from 1 portion.

GRILLED ZUCCHINI WRAPS
with sun-dried tomatoes

SERVES 2
PREP 5 MINS
COOK 4–6 MINS

2 **zucchini**, cut into ¼in
  (5mm) slices lengthwise
2 tbsp **olive oil**
2 large **flour tortillas** (vegan)
6 tbsp **hummus**
8 pieces **sun-dried tomatoes**
  in oil, drained and chopped,
  oil reserved
handful of **arugula**
lemon juice
freshly ground **black pepper**

1 Preheat a grill pan. Brush the zucchini slices with olive oil, then grill for 2–3 minutes on each side or until tender and striped brown. Set aside.

2 Put the tortillas on a board and spread with the hummus. Lay the zucchini strips on top and scatter with the sun-dried tomatoes.

3 Scatter the arugula on top, drizzle with the tomato oil and a squeeze of lemon juice, then add a good grinding of pepper. Fold in the sides, roll up each tightly, and cut in half.

the good stuff

Zucchini offers high levels of antioxidants and vitamin C. They also have anti-inflammatory properties. A protein-packed chickpea hummus is the perfect spread or dip for a vegan diet.

flex it

Meat-eaters can add some
thinly sliced roasted chicken
to this wrap if they want
to change it up.

CRISPY EGGPLANT SUBS
with Italian herb seasoning

MAKES 4
PREP 15 MINS
COOK 15 MINS, plus draining

½ tsp **sea salt**
1 large **eggplant**, sliced lengthwise
    in ¼in (5mm) slices
½ cup **all-purpose flour**
½ cup **breadcrumbs**
2 tbsp **Italian herb seasoning**
1 tsp **garlic salt**
2 tbsp **olive oil**, plus extra olive oil
    (or grapeseed oil), for frying
4 x 6in (15cm) **sub rolls** (vegan),
    sliced horizontally
1 **garlic clove**, halved
2 **tomatoes**, sliced
3 cups **romaine** or **iceberg lettuce**,
    shredded
½ small **red onion**, sliced paper thin
hot peppadew or **hot cherry**
    peppers, drained and sliced
    (optional)
2 tbsp **red wine vinegar**

1 Sprinkle the sea salt over the eggplant slices, place these in a colander, and set aside to drain for 10 minutes. Pat the slices dry, squeezing gently to remove any bitter liquid.

2 In 3 separate shallow bowls, place ½ cup of water; the all-purpose flour; and the breadcrumbs, Italian herb seasoning, and garlic salt.

3 Coat the eggplant slices in the following manner: dip each slice first in the water, then in the flour; quickly dip in the water again, followed by the breadcrumbs. Dredge one last time in flour, and shake off any excess. Set aside each breaded slice, and continue until all slices are coated in this way.

4 In a large frying pan over medium-high heat, heat enough olive oil (or grapeseed oil) to come ¼in (5mm) up the side of the pan for shallow frying. When the oil shimmers, add the eggplant slices a few at a time, taking care not to crowd the pan. Fry for about 2 minutes or until golden and crispy, turn over the slices, and fry the other side until golden. Set the cooked slices aside on a kitchen-paper-lined baking sheet and repeat until all the eggplant has been fried.

5 Heat a grill to high, place the split sub rolls on a baking sheet, and toast for 2–3 minutes or until golden. Rub the toasted rolls with the cut garlic clove, and drizzle them evenly with the 2 tablespoons of olive oil.

6 To assemble the sandwiches, evenly divide the eggplant slices among the rolls. Top with the tomato, shredded lettuce, and red onion slices, again evenly distributing the ingredients. Place a few hot pepper slices (if using) on each sandwich, drizzle with the red wine vinegar, and serve.

OYSTER MUSHROOM PO'BOYS
with plant-based mayonnaise dressing

MAKES 4
PREP 15 MINS
COOK 5 MINS

4 tbsp **plant-based mayonnaise**
1 tbsp **tomato ketchup**
1 tbsp grated **sweet onion**
1 tbsp **pickled cucumber relish**
1 tsp finely chopped **chives**
1 cup **all-purpose flour**
1¼ cups **fine polenta**
  (or cornmeal)
¾lb (340g) **oyster mushrooms**,
  pulled apart into chunks
grapeseed oil, for frying
1 tsp **Old Bay seasoning**
½ tsp **sweet paprika**
4 x 6in (15cm) soft **sub rolls** (vegan),
  sliced horizontally
2 cups **iceberg lettuce**,
  shredded
lemon wedges, to serve

1 In a small bowl, make the dressing by combining the plant-based mayonnaise, ketchup, sweet onion, relish, and chives. Refrigerate until ready to use. (This dressing can be made up to 3 days in advance.)

2 In 3 separate shallow bowls, place ½ cup of water, all-purpose flour, and polenta.

3 Coat the oyster mushrooms as follows: dip each first in the water, then in the flour; quickly dip in the water again, and then dredge thoroughly in polenta. Set aside each mushroom, and continue until all the mushrooms are coated in this way.

4 In a large frying pan over medium heat, heat enough grapeseed oil to come ¾in (2cm) up the sides of the pan.

5 Add the breaded mushrooms to the frying pan, and fry for about 3 minutes, turning once or twice, until golden on all sides. Drain on paper towels, and sprinkle with Old Bay seasoning and sweet paprika.

6 Pile the mushrooms generously onto the sub rolls, drizzle each sandwich with about 1 tablespoon of dressing, top with the iceberg lettuce, and serve the lemon wedges on the side.

the good stuff

Oyster mushrooms provide the B vitamins riboflavin and niacin, which are especially important for people who don't eat meat. They are also a good source of selenium and potassium.

flex it

For a meaty twist, layer 1oz (30g) cooked, chopped chicken or pork on top of the sweet potato when you are filling the tortillas.

QUESADILLAS
with pinto beans & sweet potato

MAKES 4
PREP 20 MINS
COOK 40 MINS

1 small **sweet potato**, peeled
2 tbsp **vegetable oil**
1 **jalapeño chile**, seeded
   and diced
4 large **flour tortillas** (vegan)
2 cups finely grated
   Cheddar-style cheese
   (vegan)
1 cup cooked **pinto** or
   borlotti beans
½ cup chopped **scallions**
1 cup chopped **cilantro**
   leaves
plant-based sour cream,
   to serve

1 With the medium blade of a spiralizer, spiralize the sweet potato.

2 In a medium frying pan, heat the vegetable oil over medium-low heat until shimmering. Add the jalapeño and cook for 3 minutes, or until tender but not brown. Add the sweet potato and cook for 7 minutes, or until just al dente.

3 To assemble, place 1 tortilla on a clean, flat surface. Sprinkle about ¼ cup of the vegan cheese on the lower half of the tortilla. Top with a quarter of the pinto beans and a quarter of the sweet potato. Add 2 tablespoons of scallions and 2 tablespoons of cilantro. Top with another ¼ cup cheese, then fold over the top of the tortilla to create a semicircle. Repeat to make 4 quesadillas in total.

4 Heat a nonstick frying pan over medium heat. Add 1 quesadilla and cook for 4 minutes. Carefully turn, cover, and cook for another 4 minutes, until the tortilla is golden and the cheese melted. Repeat for the remaining 3 quesadillas.

5 Cut each quesadilla into 4 sections. Serve immediately with plant-based sour cream on the side.

the good stuff

Sweet potatoes are packed with vitamin C, potassium, and calcium, and they also contain a load of beta-carotene, which helps reduce the appearance of aging due to the powerful antioxidants in carotenoids.

PASTA & NOODLES

flex it

If you want to add a little meat, top this pasta dish with 5½oz (150g) of cooked crispy pancetta cubes.

FARFALLE
with spinach, avocado, & tomatoes

SERVES 4
PREP 10 MINS
COOK 20 MINS

14oz (400g) **egg-free farfalle**
2 tbsp **olive oil**
4 **scallions**, cut into
   short lengths
1 **garlic clove**, finely chopped
1 tsp **crushed dried chiles**
1 × 12oz (350g) pkg **baby
   spinach leaves**
⅔ cup **vegetable stock**
4 **slow-roasted
   tomatoes**, chopped
¾ cup **baby plum
   tomatoes**, halved
4 tbsp **black olives**,
   pitted and sliced
1½ tbsp **pickled capers**
2 **avocados**, diced
squeeze of **lemon juice**
salt and freshly ground
   black pepper
3 tbsp **pumpkin seeds**
lemon wedges, to garnish
torn **basil leaves**, to garnish

1 Cook the farfalle according to the package instructions, then drain. Heat the olive oil in a deep-sided sauté pan or wok. Add the scallions and garlic and fry, stirring gently, for 1 minute. Stir in the chiles.

2 Add the spinach and vegetable stock and simmer, turning over gently, for about 2 minutes, until the spinach begins to wilt. Gently fold in the pasta and the remaining ingredients. Simmer for 3 minutes until most of the liquid has been absorbed.

3 Pile into warmed, shallow bowls. Garnish with lemon wedges and a few torn basil leaves.

the good stuff

Spinach has outstanding health benefits; it is full of carotenoids and vitamin K. Thanks to its high levels of thylakoid, it can also help you curb hunger cravings.

CREAMY PASTA
with swiss chard & tomatoes

SERVES 4
PREP 5 MINS
COOK 15 MINS

1lb (450g) **egg-free fettuccine**
4 tbsp **extra virgin olive oil**
3 **garlic cloves**, thinly sliced
bunch of **Swiss chard**, washed
  well and torn into small pieces
½ tsp **sea salt**
2 large **tomatoes**, cored,
  seeded, and cut into
  ¼in (5mm) strips
8 tbsp **plant-based sour cream**
½ tsp **crushed chiles**

1 Cook the fettuccine in boiling, well-salted water according to the package instructions.

2 Meanwhile, heat the olive oil in a large frying pan over medium heat. Add the garlic and cook, stirring, for 30 seconds.

3 Add the Swiss chard and sea salt, and cook, stirring once or twice or until tender. Remove from the heat and cover to keep warm while the pasta finishes cooking.

4 When the pasta is ready, reserve ½ cup cooking water and drain the pasta. Add the pasta to the Swiss chard, along with the tomatoes, plant-based sour cream, and crushed chiles. Toss well, adding a little reserved pasta water if needed, and serve immediately.

the good stuff

Swiss chard is another dark green leafy veggie that should be included in a vegan diet, as it is chock full of vitamins C, A, K, and B6, and important minerals, such as magnesium, iron, manganese, copper, and potassium.

flex it

Nonvegans, treat yourself with a sprinkling of freshly grated Parmesan cheese on top to serve.

SPICED EGGPLANT LINGUINE
with chili & oregano

SERVES 4
PREP 15 MINS
COOK 25 MINS

6 tbsp **olive oil**
2 **onions**, peeled and
   finely chopped
2 **eggplants**, 1 cut into ½in
   (1cm) dice, the other grated
4 **garlic cloves**, peeled
   and chopped
½ tsp **chili flakes**
2⅛ cups **tomato purée**
1 tsp **dried oregano**
salt and freshly ground
   black pepper
14oz (400g) **egg-free linguine**

1 Pour the olive oil into a large frying pan and heat. Add the onion and cook over low heat for 3 minutes until soft, then add the diced eggplant and cook for 3 minutes more. Add the grated eggplant, garlic, and chili flakes and cook for another 3 minutes. Pour in the tomato purée, add the oregano, and season well with salt and pepper. Bring to a simmer and allow to cook, uncovered, for 15 minutes.

2 Meanwhile, add the linguine to a large pan of boiling salted water and cook for 8–10 minutes, or according to package instructions. Drain and return to the pan.

3 Add half the eggplant mixture to the pasta and toss, then transfer to a large serving dish, or individual dishes, and top with the remaining sauce.

the good stuff

Garlic is a good way of adding flavor without piling on the salt. Eggplants contain an impressive array of vitamins and minerals, including high levels of fiber, folate, potassium, and manganese, as well as vitamins C, K, and B6, phosphorus, copper, thiamine, and magnesium.

VERMICELLI RICE NOODLES
with wasabi dressing

SERVES 2
PREP 15 MINS

2¼oz (70g) **dried vermicelli rice noodles**
⅔ cup **sugar snap peas**, finely sliced lengthwise
4 **radishes**, finely sliced
finely grated zest of ½ **lime**, plus ½ **lime**, peeled, segmented, and chopped
1 tbsp **unsalted pistachios**, roughly chopped
a few **basil leaves** (optional)
handful of **cilantro leaves** (optional)
lime wedges (optional)

WASABI DRESSING
1 cup **spinach leaves**
3 tbsp **silken tofu**
1 **garlic clove**, halved
juice of ½ **lemon**
sea salt and freshly ground **black pepper**
1–2 tsp **wasabi**, to taste

1 Put the vermicelli rice noodles in a bowl and cover with boiling water. Leave for 5 minutes (or according to the package instructions), then drain and set aside.

2 Meanwhile, make the dressing by putting the spinach leaves in a food processor and blending until chopped. Spoon in the silken tofu; add the garlic, lemon juice, and sea salt and pepper to taste; and blend again. Add the wasabi a little at a time, tasting and adding more wasabi or seasoning as needed, and blend until puréed. Spoon the dressing into a bowl. (This makes 4 servings. Store the extra servings in an airtight container in the refrigerator for up to 3 days.)

3 Mix the sugar snap peas, radishes, and lime zest in a bowl, season with salt and pepper, then toss with a little of the wasabi dressing.

4 Transfer the noodles to a serving bowl, then add the lime segments. Spoon in the sugar snap pea mixture and the remaining dressing, then sprinkle with the unsalted pistachios, basil leaves, and cilantro leaves (if using) and add the lime wedges (if using), to squeeze over the bowl.

the good stuff

Naturally sweet sugar snap peas are perfect for eating raw. They also make a good snack on their own, as they are high in vitamin C and low in calories.

flex it

A few juicy cooked jumbo shrimp work well scattered over this dish for those who eat seafood.

flex it

For a salty nonvegan kick, stir through 1 tablespoon of chopped anchovies just before serving.

ONE-PAN PASTA PRIMAVERA
with broccoli, spinach, & peas

SERVES 4
PREP 10 MINS
COOK 20 MINS

4 tbsp **extra virgin olive oil**

1 **onion**, halved and thinly sliced

2 **garlic cloves**, thinly sliced

12oz (350g) **egg-free thin spaghetti**

3½ cups **vegetable stock** or **water**

1 × 14oz (400g) can **chopped tomatoes**, with juice

¾ cup **fresh** or **frozen broccoli florets**

1 **carrot**, peeled, halved, and thinly sliced

1 tsp **sea salt**

3⅓ cups **baby spinach**

½ cup **fresh** or **frozen baby peas**

½ tsp freshly ground **black pepper**

1 Heat the olive oil in an extra-large frying pan with a lid over medium-high heat. Add the onion and sauté for 2 minutes.

2 Add the garlic, spaghetti, vegetable stock, tomatoes with their juice, broccoli, carrot, and sea salt. Bring to a boil, reduce the heat to medium-low, cover, and cook for 3 minutes.

3 Uncover, stir, and continue cooking, stirring constantly and adjusting the heat as necessary to maintain a brisk simmer, for about 8 minutes or until the stock is absorbed and the pasta is tender.

4 Stir in the baby spinach, peas, and black pepper, toss for 1 minute, and serve immediately.

the good stuff

The greater the variety of vegetables you eat, the better for your health. Here, you get your daily servings with a load of vitamin-rich veggies in one pan.

RAINBOW LENTIL MEATBALLS
with arrabbiata sauce

SERVES 4
PREP 20 MINS
COOK 45 MINS

1½ cups cooked **red lentils**,
   thoroughly drained
½ cup cooked **brown lentils**,
   thoroughly drained
3 tbsp **aquafaba** (water from
   a can of chickpeas/beans),
   lightly beaten
¾ cup **panko breadcrumbs**
½ tsp **garlic powder**
1 tsp **dried oregano**
zest of 1 large **lemon**
¼ tsp ground **cayenne pepper**
14oz (400g) **egg-free spaghetti**
vegan Parmesan, to serve
   (optional)

ARRABBIATA SAUCE
2 tbsp **olive oil**
1 small **onion**, finely chopped
2 x 14oz (400g) cans
   chopped tomatoes
1 tbsp crushed **dried chiles**
salt and freshly ground
   black pepper

1 Preheat the oven to 350°F (180°C). Lightly oil a baking sheet. In a large mixing bowl, combine the red lentils, brown lentils, aquafaba, panko breadcrumbs, garlic powder, oregano, lemon zest, and cayenne pepper.

2 With your hands, form approximately 1 tablespoon of the lentil mixture into a meatball and place on the baking sheet. Repeat with the remaining mixture. Bake for 25 minutes, rotating the meatballs halfway through.

3 Meanwhile, to make the arrabbiata sauce, in a saucepan, warm the olive oil over medium-low heat. Add the onion and cook for 2 minutes, or until soft. Add the tomatoes and chiles. Simmer over low heat for 15 minutes, or until the sauce is warmed through. Season with salt and pepper to taste.

4 While the sauce is simmering, add the spaghetti to a large pan of boiling salted water and cook for 8–10 minutes or according to package instructions. Drain and return to the pan.

5 Place the pasta and meatballs on 4 plates, top with the sauce, and serve immediately.

the good stuff

This dish is loaded with protein and fiber from the health-bursting lentils and vitamin C-rich canned tomatoes—both are a must for the vegan pantry.

flex it

An extra treat for nonvegans:
sprinkle some dairy
Parmesan cheese over
the pasta and meatballs
to serve.

LEMON, GARLIC, & PARSLEY LINGUINE
with hot chili flakes

SERVES 4
PREP 5 MINS
COOK 10 MINS

12oz (350g) **egg-free linguine**
3 tbsp **olive oil**
2 **garlic cloves**, finely chopped
zest of ½ **lemon** and juice of
   1 **lemon**
handful of **flat-leaf parsley**,
   finely chopped
pinch of **chili flakes** (optional)
salt and freshly ground
   black pepper

1 Add the linguine to a large pan of salted boiling water and cook for 8–10 minutes or according to the instructions on the package. Drain, then return to the pan with a little of the cooking water and toss together.

2 While the pasta is cooking, heat the olive oil in a frying pan, add the garlic, and cook on very low heat, being very careful not to burn it. Cook for about 1 minute, then add the lemon zest and juice and cook for a couple more minutes.

3 Stir in the parsley and chili flakes, if using. Season with salt and black pepper, then add the mixture to the pasta and toss to coat. A tomato and basil salad would work well with this dish.

the good stuff

Parsley not only acts as a flavor enhancer and garnish here. It is good to add to your food instead of salt, as it's full of vitamin K—a small bunch will provide almost all of your daily intake.

UDON NOODLES WITH SWEET & SOUR TOFU
& pickled ginger

SERVES 4
PREP 5 MINS
COOK 10 MINS

9oz (250g) **firm tofu**, cut into cubes
2 tbsp **sunflower oil**
1 tbsp **pickled ginger**
salt and freshly ground
    black pepper
10oz (300g) **egg-free udon
    noodles**

SWEET & SOUR SAUCE
1 tbsp **sunflower oil**
3 **garlic cloves**, finely chopped
1 × 2in (5cm) piece of **fresh ginger**,
    cut into fine strips
pinch of **light brown sugar**
10 **cherry tomatoes**, halved
4 **scallions**, finely chopped
1 tbsp **dark soy sauce**
1 tbsp **rice vinegar**
1 tbsp **Chinese cooking wine**

1 First, make the sauce. Pour 1 tablespoon of sunflower oil into a
wok, then add the garlic and fresh ginger and cook for 1 minute.
Tip in the brown sugar and stir for a few seconds, then add the tomatoes
and scallions. Keep stirring for a few more minutes, until the tomatoes
start to break down. (You can squash them with the back of a fork.)

2 Add the soy sauce, rice vinegar, and Chinese cooking wine. Bring
to a boil, reduce to a simmer, and cook for a couple of minutes.

3 Fry the tofu in 2 tablespoons of sunflower oil until golden. Stir the
tofu and pickled ginger into the sweet and sour sauce. Taste, and
season with salt and black pepper if required.

4 To finish, stir in the udon noodles and wait until they soften (about
2 minutes), then serve.

flex it

For the meat-eaters, swap
the tofu for 9oz (250g) pork
tenderloin, finely sliced, and
fry it separately with the
ingredients as
you would the tofu.

flex it

For a nonvegan treat, add some cooked, peeled shrimp to a separate portion of the sauce and heat through before tossing with the noodles.

SESAME NOODLES
with peanut butter & tahini

SERVES 4
PREP 10 MINS
COOK 15 MINS

2 tsp **sea salt**

1lb (450g) **egg-free linguine**

4 tbsp **tahini**

4 tbsp **smooth peanut butter**

2 tbsp **low-sodium tamari**
or **soy sauce**

2 tbsp **rice vinegar**

2 tbsp grated **fresh ginger**

1 tsp **toasted sesame oil**

1 tsp **chili garlic sauce**

1 **carrot**, julienned

1 **cucumber**, julienned

3 tbsp **gomasio**

4 tbsp thinly sliced **scallions**, both
light and dark green parts

1 Bring a large pan of water to a boil over medium-high heat. Add the sea salt and linguine and cook for 8–10 minutes or according to the package instructions until the pasta is tender. Drain, rinse the pasta under cold water, and set aside.

2 In a large bowl, whisk together the tahini, peanut butter, 4 tablespoons of hot water, tamari or soy sauce, rice vinegar, ginger, toasted sesame oil, and chili garlic sauce.

3 Add the cooked linguine, carrot, and cucumber to the sauce. Toss gently, garnish with gomasio and scallions, and serve immediately.

the good stuff

Tahini is a paste made from ground sesame seeds, and by using it, you'll get most of your vitamins in one hit, as it's high in vitamins E, B1, B2, B3, B5, and B15.

NO-COOK CRUNCHY STIR-FRY
with rice vinegar

SERVES 2
PREP 20 MINS

2¼oz (70g) **flat rice noodles**
1 cup **carrot**, finely sliced
1¼ cups **zucchini**, finely sliced
½ **red bell pepper**, finely sliced
¼ **red chile**, finely sliced
2 tsp **sesame seeds**
1 × 1in (2.5cm) piece of **lemongrass**,
    outer leaves removed, inner part
    finely sliced
1 cup **button mushrooms**,
    halved
1 **scallion**, trimmed, green part
    finely sliced, and white part
    sliced lengthwise
a few **purple basil leaves** (optional)

DRESSING
1 tsp **dark soy sauce**
1 tsp **rice vinegar**
juice of ½ **lime**
½ **garlic clove**, grated
½ **red chile**, finely chopped
sea salt and freshly ground
    black pepper

1 Put the flat rice noodles in a bowl and cover with boiling water. Leave for 10 minutes (or according to the package instructions), then drain and set aside.

2 Make the dressing by mixing the dark soy sauce, rice vinegar, lime juice, garlic, and red chile in a bowl, and season with salt and pepper to taste.

3 Combine the carrot, zucchini, red bell pepper, red chile, sesame seeds, lemongrass, mushrooms, and the white part of the scallion in a bowl. Add half the noodles and season with salt and pepper. Mix, trickle in the rice vinegar dressing, and mix again.

4 Transfer the no-cook stir-fry mix to a serving bowl, then add the remaining noodles. Sprinkle over the green part of the scallion and the purple basil leaves (if using), then serve.

the good stuff

Eating your vegetables raw will ensure you get optimum nutrition, as none of the good stuff is lost in the cooking process.

PULSES & GRAINS

flex it

For a nonvegan twist, add 8oz (225g) cooked, peeled shrimp along with the red bell pepper strips in step 3.

THREE-BEAN PAELLA
with peas & peppers

SERVES 6
PREP 35 MINS
COOK 1 HR 5 MINS

2 tbsp **olive oil**

1 **onion**, chopped

3 **garlic cloves**, finely chopped

pinch of **saffron threads**

pinch of **crushed dried chiles**

1¼ cups **chopped tomatoes**

1 tsp **smoked paprika**

1lb (450g) **paella rice**, such as
   Bomba or Calasparra

2½ cups **vegetable stock**

1 cup cooked **navy beans**

⅔ cup cooked **pigeon peas** or
   black-eyed peas

¾ cup cooked **kidney beans**

½ cup **frozen peas**, thawed

salt and freshly ground
   black pepper

⅔ cup **roasted red bell
   pepper strips**

2oz (60g) **green Spanish olives**,
   pitted and sliced

1 large **lemon**, cut into 8 wedges

flat-leaf parsley, to garnish

1 In a 10in (25cm) paella pan or large cast-iron frying pan, warm the olive oil over medium heat until shimmering. Add the onion and cook for 2 minutes, or until it starts to soften. Stir in the garlic and cook for 30 seconds, or until fragrant. Incorporate the saffron, dried chiles, tomatoes, and paprika. Stir in the paella rice and cook for 2–3 minutes.

2 Add the vegetable stock to the rice mixture and stir. Bring to a boil, then reduce the heat to low and cook, covered, for 20 minutes. Stir in the navy beans, pigeon peas (or black-eyed peas), and kidney beans. Cover again and cook for an additional 10 minutes. Scatter the thawed peas across the top and cook without stirring, covered, for another 10 minutes, or until the beans and peas are warmed through. Remove from the heat.

3 Season with salt and pepper to taste. Arrange the red bell pepper strips and olives evenly across the top. Cover and let the paella stand for 5 minutes. Garnish with lemon wedges and parsley, then serve.

the good stuff

Only green vegetables comes as close to beans as a valuable food source—it's important when eating a plant-based diet to aim to include beans most days.

ITALIAN TOMATO BARLEY RISOTTO
with green olives & basil

SERVES 4
PREP 10 MINS
COOK 45 MINS

1 tbsp **light olive oil**
1 **onion**, finely chopped
2 **garlic cloves**, crushed
1½ cups **pearl barley**, rinsed
1½ cups **tomato purée**
2 cups **vegetable stock**
1 tsp **Italian seasoning**
1 × 14oz (400g) can **cannellini
   beans**, drained
4¼oz (120g) **green olives**,
   pitted and halved
salt and freshly ground
   black pepper
handful of **basil leaves**, to garnish
vegan Parmesan, to serve
   (optional)

1 Heat the olive oil in a large, lidded saucepan over medium-high heat. Add the onions and garlic and cook for about 5 minutes or until the onions are softened. Then add the barley to the pan, stir to coat with the oil, and cook for another 2 minutes.

2 Add the tomato purée, vegetable stock, and Italian seasoning to the pan. Stir well and reduce the heat to a simmer. Cover and cook for 30 minutes, or until most of the liquid has been absorbed and the barley is chewy. Make sure you stir the risotto occasionally to prevent the barley from sticking to the bottom of the pan.

3 Stir the cannellini beans into the risotto and cook for another 5 minutes. Remove from the heat and stir in the olives, making sure they are evenly distributed. Season to taste, garnish with basil leaves, and serve hot.

the good stuff

Barley is a fantastic plant-based source of protein—more so than brown rice—and fiber. It is also rich in magnesium and contains iron and vitamin B6.

flex it

For a cheesy treat, nonvegan members of the household could swap the vegan Parmesan for a dairy version.

BROWN RICE RISOTTO
with red peppers & artichokes

SERVES 4
PREP 10 MINS
COOK 50 MINS–1 HR

1 tbsp **olive oil**
1 **onion**, finely chopped
salt and freshly ground
  black pepper
2 sweet **pointed red peppers**,
  halved, seeded, and chopped
pinch of **chili flakes**
1½ cups **brown rice**
3½ cups **vegetable stock**
1 × 10oz (280g) jar **artichoke hearts**,
  drained and roughly chopped
handful of **flat-leaf parsley**,
  finely chopped

1 Heat the olive oil in a large frying pan, then add the onion and cook on low heat until soft and transparent. Season with a pinch of salt and black pepper. Add the pointed red peppers and cook for a few minutes until they soften.

2 Add the chili flakes, then stir in the rice. Raise the heat a little, pour in a ladleful of the vegetable stock, and bring to a boil. Reduce to a simmer and cook gently for 40–50 minutes, adding a little more stock each time the liquid is absorbed, until the rice is cooked.

3 Stir through the artichokes and cook for a couple of minutes to heat through, then taste and season as required. Cover with a lid, remove from the heat, and leave for 10 minutes. Stir through the flat-leaf parsley and transfer to plates or bowls. You could serve this with an arugula salad on the side.

the good stuff

Just 1⅛ cups of brown rice provides tons of your daily fiber requirement. It's an important grain for a plant-based diet as it is rich in protein, thiamine, calcium, magnesium, fiber, and potassium.

SWEET POTATO & SPINACH CURRY
with ginger & cilantro

SERVES 4
PREP 10 MINS
COOK 20 MINS

2 tbsp **coconut oil**
1 **onion**, finely chopped
2 **garlic cloves**, crushed
1 × 2in (5cm) piece of **fresh ginger**, grated
1 tsp **mustard seeds**
¼ tsp **ground cinnamon**
½ tsp **ground turmeric**
½ tsp **cayenne pepper**
1 tsp **ground cumin**
1 tsp **ground coriander**
1 × 14oz (400ml) can **reduced-fat coconut milk**
1⅛ cups **vegetable stock**
3 large **sweet potatoes**, peeled and cut into 1½in (3cm) cubes, about 5¼ cups in total
3⅓ cups **baby spinach leaves**
salt, to taste
1 small handful of **cilantro leaves**, roughly chopped

1 Heat the coconut oil in a large, shallow pan. Fry the onion over medium heat for 3–4 minutes, until it has softened but is not brown. Add the garlic and ginger, and cook for another minute, then add all the remaining spices and cook over low heat for another minute, stirring constantly, until they darken slightly and start to release their fragrance.

2 Add the coconut milk and vegetable stock to the pan and mix well. Add the diced sweet potatoes and bring the mixture to a boil, then reduce to a low simmer and cook, covered, for 10–12 minutes until the potatoes are just soft.

3 Remove the lid and gently stir in the spinach leaves to avoid breaking up the sweet potatoes. The curry is ready when the spinach has wilted into the sauce, which should take about 1–2 minutes. Taste and add a little salt, if needed.

4 Remove from the heat and stir in the chopped cilantro before serving with cooked brown rice.

the good stuff

Sweet potatoes, spinach, and coconut milk make this a dish rich in vitamin C. It is flavored with superfood spices, too—mustard seeds and turmeric have anti-inflammatory properties.

flex it

For an easy nonvegan
alternative, add 7oz (200g)
cooked, peeled shrimp
in step 3.

CASHEW PAELLA
with mushrooms & paprika

SERVES 4
PREP 10 MINS
COOK 25 MINS

large pinch of **saffron strands**
2½ cups hot **vegetable stock**
2 tbsp **olive oil**
1 **leek**, chopped
1 **onion**, chopped
2 **garlic cloves**, crushed
1 **red bell pepper**, seeded and chopped
1 **carrot**, chopped
1½ cups **paella rice**
⅔ cup **dry white wine**
1⅔ cups **chestnut mushrooms**, sliced
1¾ cups **roasted, unsalted cashews**
salt and freshly ground **black pepper**
1 cup **fresh shelled** or **frozen peas**
1½ tbsp chopped **thyme**
4 **tomatoes**, quartered
½ tsp **smoked paprika**
sprig of **flat-leaf parsley**, to garnish
lemon wedges, to garnish

1 Put the saffron strands in the stock to infuse. Heat the olive oil in a paella pan or large frying pan and fry the leek, onion, garlic, red bell pepper, and carrot, stirring, for 3 minutes until softened but not browned. Add the rice and stir until coated in oil and glistening.

2 Add the white wine and boil until it has been absorbed, stirring. Stir in the saffron-infused stock, mushrooms, cashews, and some salt and pepper. Bring to a boil, stirring once, then reduce the heat, cover, and simmer very gently for 10 minutes.

3 Add the peas and thyme, stir gently, then distribute the tomatoes over the top. Cover and simmer very gently for another 10 minutes until the rice is just tender and has absorbed most of the liquid but is still creamy.

4 Sprinkle the paprika over and stir through gently, taking care not to break up the tomatoes. Taste and adjust the seasoning, if necessary.

5 Garnish with a sprig of parsley and lemon wedges and serve hot with crusty bread and a green salad.

the good stuff

Although good for you—cashews contain high levels of vitamin E, magnesium, and zinc—they are also fairly high in fat, so don't overindulge.

BUCKWHEAT STIR-FRY
with eggplant, zucchini, & kale

SERVES 4
PREP 15 MINS
COOK 20 MINS

pinch of **salt**
1 cup **buckwheat**
3 tbsp **grapeseed oil**
2 **dried red chiles**
1 **garlic clove**, thinly sliced
1 tsp grated **fresh ginger**
drizzle of **toasted sesame oil** (optional)
4 **Japanese eggplants**, cut into cubes
2 **zucchini**, cut into cubes
4 **kale leaves**, ribs removed and roughly chopped
handful of **basil leaves**, roughly chopped
sesame seeds, to garnish

MISO
2 tbsp **white miso**
1½ tsp **brown rice vinegar**
1 tsp grated **fresh ginger**

1 Place 2 cups of water in a large, lidded saucepan and add a pinch of salt. Bring to a boil, then slowly stir in the buckwheat. Reduce the heat to a simmer, cover, and cook for 15 minutes. Then remove from the heat, cover, and leave to stand.

2 Meanwhile, heat the grapeseed oil in a large frying pan over medium heat. Add the red chiles and cook for about 2 minutes, stirring, until fragrant. Add the garlic, ginger, and sesame oil, if using, and cook for 2 minutes, stirring frequently. Then add the eggplants and zucchini and cook for another 8–10 minutes, stirring frequently, until the vegetables are cooked through.

3 Meanwhile, for the miso, place all the ingredients in a bowl, add 1 teaspoon of water, and mix until well combined. Stir the mixture into the vegetables and mix well to coat. Then add the kale and cook for another 2–3 minutes, until just wilted. Remove from the heat and sprinkle over the basil leaves and sesame seeds. Serve hot over the buckwheat.

the good stuff

This colorful dish introduces a variety of healthy vegetables such as kale, which is high in iron, as well as healthy and filling buckwheat, which is rich in manganese and magnesium.

TOFU STIR-FRY
with kamut

SERVES 2
PREP 15 MINS, plus
marinating and soaking
COOK 1 HR

14oz (400g) **firm tofu**,
drained and cubed
½ cup **raw kamut**
3 tbsp **vegetable oil**
1 **carrot**, cut into sticks
1 **red bell pepper**, seeded
and thinly sliced
¼ cup **bean sprouts**

4 **scallions**,
thinly sliced
salt and freshly ground
black pepper

MARINADE
4 tbsp **soy sauce**
2 tbsp **maple syrup**
1 × 2in (5cm) piece of
fresh ginger, finely
chopped
2 **garlic cloves**,
finely chopped

1 Combine the marinade ingredients in a bowl.
Place the tofu in a plastic bag along with half
the marinade. Seal, and shake to coat. Marinate in
the refrigerator for 3–4 hours. Reserve the marinade.

2 Place the kamut in a bowl, cover with water, and
soak for 8 hours. Rinse and drain, then place in a
lidded saucepan. Cover with water and bring to a
boil. Simmer for 45 minutes or until tender. Drain.

3 Heat 2 tablespoons of oil in a frying pan over
medium-high heat. Sauté the tofu for 10 minutes,
until browned. Remove with a slotted spoon. Add
the remaining oil to the pan and cook the carrots
and peppers for 2 minutes, stirring frequently. Then
add the bean sprouts and cook for 3 minutes, stirring.
Stir in the kamut, tofu, and reserved marinade. Add
the scallions and cook for 2 minutes. Season to taste.

THAI STIR-FRY
with wheat berries

SERVES 2
PREP 10 MINS
COOK 1 HR

½ cup **wheat berries**
2 tbsp **smooth
peanut butter**
2 tbsp **maple syrup**
1 tbsp **soy sauce**
¼ tsp **chili flakes**
juice of 1 **lime**
1 tbsp **vegetable oil**
⅓ cup **bean sprouts**

¾ cup **green
cabbage**, shredded
1 **carrot**, sliced
into matchsticks
½ cup **soybeans**
salt and freshly ground
black pepper
2 tbsp roughly chopped
cilantro leaves

1 Place the wheat berries in a pan, cover with
water, and bring to a boil. Reduce the heat to
a simmer, cover, and cook for 45–50 minutes, until
tender. Remove from the heat and drain any
remaining water.

2 Place the peanut butter, maple syrup, soy
sauce, and chili flakes in a bowl and stir to
combine. Then add the lime juice and mix until it
forms a smooth sauce. Heat the vegetable oil in a
large frying pan over high heat. Add the bean
sprouts, cabbage, and carrots and stir-fry for
3–5 minutes. Then add the soybeans and wheat
berries and stir-fry for another 2 minutes. Pour
over the peanut sauce and toss to coat. Season
to taste and remove from the heat. Sprinkle with
cilantro and serve hot.

VEGETABLE STIR-FRY
with sprouted quinoa & sesame

SERVES 2
PREP 10 MINS
COOK 5 MINS

2 tbsp **vegetable oil**

2 tsp **sesame oil**

1 **carrot**, peeled and julienned

¼ **red onion**, finely sliced

½ **zucchini**, julienned

½ cup **sprouted mung beans**

¾ cup **Savoy cabbage**,
finely shredded

2 tbsp finely chopped **fresh
ginger**

2 **garlic cloves**, crushed or
finely chopped

1 **jalapeño** or **other chile**, seeded
and finely chopped

1lb (450g) **sprouted quinoa**

2 tbsp **sprouted sesame seeds**

2 tbsp **low-sodium soy sauce**

1 Heat a wok or large frying pan over high heat and add the vegetable oil and sesame oil. When the oil has almost begun to smoke, add the carrot, and stir-fry for 1 minute. Add the red onion and zucchini and cook for another minute. Add the sprouted mung beans, cabbage, ginger, garlic, and jalapeño and cook for 1 minute more.

2 Add the sprouted quinoa and sesame seeds to the vegetables, and cook over high heat, turning constantly, until the quinoa begins to brown, about 2 minutes. Add the soy sauce to the pan and cook for a final minute before serving immediately.

the good stuff

Sprouting may increase the grains' essential nutrients—an impressive list of B vitamins, vitamin C, folate, soluble fiber, and amino acids. As these sprouts are only lightly cooked, it's best to avoid serving this salad to children and pregnant women—raw sprouted seeds, grains, and pulses carry a risk of foodborne bacteria.

CHERRY & PISTACHIO FREEKEH PILAF
with lemon dressing

SERVES 4
PREP 5 MINS
COOK 20–25 MINS

1⅛ cups **freekeh**
8 **cardamom pods**
8 **whole cloves**
1 tbsp **olive oil**
1 **onion**, finely chopped
1 tsp **ground cinnamon**
pinch of **salt**
⅔ cup **dried cherries**,
   roughly chopped
¾ cup **pistachios**,
   roughly chopped

LEMON DRESSING
3 tbsp **olive oil**
2 tbsp **lemon juice**
pinch of **salt**

1 Place the freekeh in a large saucepan, cover with 3½ cups of water, and place over medium heat. Add the cardamom and cloves and simmer for 20 minutes or until all the water has been absorbed. Drain any remaining water, then remove and discard the cardamom pods and cloves. Set aside.

2 Meanwhile, heat the olive oil in a large frying pan over medium heat. Add the onions to the pan and cook for 5–10 minutes, stirring occasionally, until softened and translucent. Then add the cinnamon and cook for another 2 minutes.

3 For the lemon dressing, place all the ingredients in a small bowl and stir to combine.

4 Add the freekeh to the onion mixture, season with the salt, and stir to mix. Then add the cherries and pistachios and stir until evenly distributed. Remove from the heat. Serve hot with the dressing drizzled over.

the good stuff

Adding dried cherries to your plant-based diet will increase your intake of copper and essential minerals.

ROASTED ROOTS & PULSES BOWL
with kale & walnuts

SERVES 2
PREP 15 MINS
COOK 40 MINS

3½oz (100g) **beets**
3½oz (100g) **carrot**
3½oz (100g) **celeriac**
3½oz (100g) **sweet potato**
1 tbsp **olive oil**
½ tsp **ground cumin**
salt and **pepper** to taste
½ cup cooked **chickpeas**
1 **garlic clove**, crushed
pinch of **cayenne pepper**
2 tbsp plus 1½ tsp **Puy lentils**
   or **green lentils**
2 tbsp **quinoa**, rinsed
¼ cup **kale leaves**, chopped
½ cup **arugula**
1 tbsp **walnut pieces**
1 tsp **pumpkin seeds**

DRESSING
1 tbsp **olive oil**
1 tsp **wholegrain mustard**
2 tsp **maple syrup**

1 Preheat the oven to 350°F (180°C). Leaving the skins on, wash and chop the beets, carrot, celeriac, and sweet potato into equal-sized chunks. Place each of the 4 root vegetables in its own quarter of a large roasting pan and drizzle over ½ tablespoon of the olive oil. Sprinkle with cumin and season with salt and pepper.

2 Place the chickpeas in a roasting pan with the garlic and ½ tablespoon of olive oil. Season with salt, pepper, and the pinch of cayenne pepper. Place both pans in the oven. Cook the chickpeas for 15 minutes and the root vegetables for 25 minutes.

3 Rinse the lentils and place in a pan. Cover with water and bring to a boil. Reduce the heat and simmer, covered, for 10 minutes. Add the quinoa and cook for 5 minutes. Steam the kale over the lentils and quinoa for 5 minutes, until it wilts. Drain the lentils and quinoa.

4 For the dressing, whisk up the olive oil, mustard, and maple syrup.

5 Layer up the lentils and quinoa, root vegetables, arugula, kale, and chickpeas in a bowl. Sprinkle with walnuts and pumpkin seeds, then drizzle with the dressing.

the good stuff

Root veggies are packed with vitamins, especially A and C, and should be included in a vegan diet, especially in the winter when our body craves vitamin C. They are also a good form of fiber.

flex it

Nonvegans can get an extra protein and calcium fix by adding ⅓ cup crumbled feta cheese over the top.

BROWN RICE SUSHI BOWL
with sprouted seeds & pickled radishes

SERVES 1
PREP 15 MINS, plus chilling
COOK 20 MINS

¾ cup **sprouted short-grain brown rice**
1 tbsp **rice wine vinegar**
¼ tsp **granulated sugar**
¼ tsp **salt**
1 tbsp **sprouted pumpkin seeds**
1 tbsp **sprouted sunflower seeds**
1 tbsp **sprouted sesame seeds**
⅕oz (5g) **dried seaweed sheets**
1 × 1in (2.5cm) piece of **cucumber**, halved, seeded, and finely sliced
½ **small avocado**, sliced

PICKLED RADISHES
½ cup **rice wine vinegar**
3 tbsp **granulated sugar**
1 tsp **fine sea salt**
4 **watermelon radishes**, washed, trimmed, and finely sliced

1 To make the pickled radishes, whisk together the vinegar, sugar, and sea salt in a small bowl until the sugar has dissolved. Pack the radishes into a small mason jar, pour the vinegar mixture over them until completely covered, and seal. Refrigerate for at least 1 hour before using. (These will keep in the refrigerator for up to 1 week.)

2 Place the sprouted brown rice in a medium heavy-based saucepan and cover with 1 cup of cold water. Bring to a boil, then reduce the heat to a simmer and cook, covered, for 15–20 minutes, until all the water has evaporated and the rice is nearly tender.

3 Put the vinegar, sugar, and salt in a small saucepan and heat, whisking, until the sugar is just dissolved. Mix the dressing into the rice and let it sit, covered, for 5 minutes.

4 Mix the sprouted pumpkin seeds, sunflower seeds, and sesame seeds into the warm rice. Set aside 1–2 of the seaweed sheets and crumble the rest over the rice. Mix well to combine.

5 Turn the warm rice mixture into a serving bowl and top it with the cucumber, avocado, and a few slices of the pickled radishes. Crumble the remaining seaweed sheets over the top and serve.

the good stuff

Seaweed is more nutrient-dense than any other land vegetable. It provides mounds of nutrients and a rich supply of minerals, mainly calcium—especially good for vegans, as they exclude dairy.

MILLET BUDDHA BOWL
with beet hummus

SERVES 1
PREP 15 MINS, plus soaking
COOK 45 MINS

¼ cup **millet**
1 **corn on the cob**
small handful of **baby spinach**
handful of **pea shoots** (or **baby salad leaves**)
¼ cup cooked **cannellini beans**
2 **chestnut mushrooms**, sliced
1 small **carrot**, julienned or grated
½ small **mango**, peeled and diced
1 tbsp **sunflower seeds**
2 **lime** wedges, to garnish

BEET HUMMUS
¾ cup **beets**, roughly chopped
½ tbsp **olive oil**, plus extra for drizzling
juice of ½ **lemon**
salt and freshly ground **black pepper**

DRESSING
1 tbsp **olive oil**
2 tsp **balsamic vinegar**

1 Soak the millet overnight in double the volume of water. Drain and rinse well.

2 For the beet hummus, preheat the oven to 350°F (180°C). Place the beets in a roasting pan, drizzle with some oil, and roast for 30 minutes until soft. Then add to a blender and blend. With the motor running, drizzle in the olive oil and add 1–3 tablespoons of water until the desired consistency is reached. Season to taste with lemon juice, salt, and pepper.

3 Place the millet in a small saucepan, cover with water, and bring to a boil. Lower the heat and simmer for 10 minutes until soft but not mushy. Drain and place in a mixing bowl.

4 Using a sharp knife, slice the corn kernels off the cob and combine with the cooked millet.

5 To make the dressing, combine the olive oil and balsamic vinegar in a small dish or glass jar and whisk or shake well.

6 Put a bed of millet and corn in a bowl and arrange the pea shoots, beans, vegetables, and mango around it with a generous dollop of beet hummus in the middle.

7 Drizzle with the dressing, sprinkle with sunflower seeds, and garnish with lime wedges. Season with salt and pepper.

the good stuff

It's hard to beat beets as a healthy food; they're rich in nitrates, vitamin C, and iron, and a great source of lysine—an essential amino acid that your body can't produce on its own.

SALADS & SIDES

flex it

For a nonvegan flavor kick, crumble over some piquant goat cheese just before serving.

LENTIL & CAULIFLOWER TABBOULEH
with mint & lemon

SERVES 4
PREP 20 MINS

1 small **cauliflower head**
¼ cup chopped **flat-leaf parsley**
½ cup chopped **curly parsley**
1⅓ cups **cucumber**, diced
1 cup **tomato**, diced
1 small bunch **scallions**,
  finely sliced
⅔ cup cooked **brown lentils**
3 tbsp chopped **mint leaves**
zest and juice of 2 **lemons**
2 tbsp **olive oil**
salt and freshly ground
  black pepper

1 Remove the outer leaves from the cauliflower head and break it into florets. Place it in a food processor and pulse 6–7 times, until the cauliflower resembles rice.

2 In a large mixing bowl, combine the cauliflower, flat-leaf parsley, curly parsley, cucumber, tomato, scallions, lentils, and mint. Add the lemon zest and juice and the olive oil and toss to combine. Season with salt and pepper to taste. Transfer to a serving dish and serve immediately.

VARIATION

For a zingy variation, add finely chopped red bell peppers, red onion, and chopped black olives into the mix in Step 2. Top with pomegranate seeds.

the good stuff

Using cauliflower as a grain is a great way to add nutrition and flavor to a dish. Cauliflower contains almost every vitamin you need, including vitamins C and B6, so it is great for a plant-based diet.

MEXICAN QUINOA SALAD
with beans & avocado

SERVES 2
PREP 15 MINS, plus cooling
COOK 20 MINS

⅓ cup **quinoa**

1 × 14oz (400g) can **red kidney beans**, drained

1 × 2oz (50g) can **sweetcorn**, drained

½ **red onion**, finely chopped

1 **red bell pepper**, seeded and finely chopped

4–6 slices pickled **jalapeño chiles**, finely chopped

1 **avocado**, pitted and cut into cubes

1 head of **romaine lettuce**

1 cup plain **corn tortilla chips**, crumbled, plus extra to serve

1 **lemon** or **lime**, halved, to serve

1 Rinse the quinoa under running water, drain, and place in a lidded saucepan. Cover with 1⅛ cups water and bring to a boil.

2 Reduce the heat to a simmer, cover, and cook for 15–20 minutes or until almost all the liquid has been absorbed and the quinoa is fluffy. Remove from the heat, drain any remaining water, and set aside to cool.

3 Place the quinoa, kidney beans, sweetcorn, onion, bell pepper, and jalapeños in a large bowl. Mix until well combined. Then add the avocado and mix gently to combine.

4 Roughly shred the lettuce and add to the bowl. Sprinkle the tortilla chips over the salad and toss lightly. Transfer to a serving platter or plate. Serve immediately with tortilla chips and lemons or limes to squeeze over.

the good stuff

Healthy eating guidelines tell us to eat a rainbow of foods for optimum nutrition—this dish will help you do just that with its colorful veggies and high-protein beans and quinoa. Quinoa also has all the essential amino acids the body needs, so it is a must-have food on a vegan diet.

flex it

Grill some chile-spiced shrimp to serve up alongside this salad for those who eat seafood.

flex it

Make this irresistible to meat-eaters by scattering over some cooked chopped sausage.

BLOOD ORANGE & BEET SALAD
with fennel & walnuts

SERVES 4
PREP 20 MINS
COOK 30 MINS

2 medium-sized **beets**, peeled
1 tbsp **olive oil**
salt and freshly ground
   black pepper
¼ cup **walnuts**,
   roughly chopped
2 small **blood oranges**
1 small **fennel bulb**, trimmed
2¼ cups **watercress**, washed
   and dried
3¾ cups **baby arugula**,
   washed and dried

DRESSING
4 tbsp **extra virgin olive oil**
1 tsp **Dijon mustard**
salt and freshly ground
   black pepper

1 Preheat the oven to 400°F (200°C). Cut the beets into thin wedges, about 8 pieces per beet, and toss in the olive oil. Season well with salt and pepper, then roast for 30 minutes, turning once, until softened and charred at the edges. Set aside to cool.

2 Dry-fry the walnut pieces for 2–3 minutes over medium heat, stirring constantly, until browned in places. Set aside to cool.

3 Prepare the blood oranges by peeling with a small, sharp knife, being careful to remove all the white pith. Use the knife to cut out each segment, leaving the dividing pith behind. Squeeze all the remaining juice out of the leftover orange "skeleton" into a bowl. Repeat with the second orange, setting the segments aside.

4 To make the dressing, add the olive oil, Dijon mustard, and seasoning to the extracted orange juice, and whisk well to combine. Slice the fennel very finely and toss it in the dressing immediately, to stop it from discoloring.

5 Toss the watercress and arugula with the fennel and dressing, then place on a large serving platter and top with the roasted beets, blood orange segments, and toasted walnuts. Serve immediately.

the good stuff

This sweet crunchy salad is high in potassium and vitamin C from the oranges, beets, fennel, and watercress, creating a super-charged meal that will keep your immune system healthy. Walnuts not only add flavor but are full of plant-based omega-3 fats.

ASIAN-STYLE SALAD
with sprouted mung beans & mint

SERVES 1
PREP 10 MINS

½ **zucchini**, spiralized

1 × 3in (8cm) piece of **cucumber**, spiralized

¼ cup **sprouted mung beans**

2 cups **pea shoots**

a few thin slices of **red onion**, to taste

2 tbsp roughly chopped **mint leaves**, plus extra to serve (optional)

1 tbsp roughly chopped **salted peanuts**

DRESSING

2 tbsp **rice wine vinegar**

2 tsp **granulated sugar**

1 tsp **sesame oil**

½ tsp **soy sauce** or **tamari**

¼ tsp finely grated **fresh ginger**

¼ tsp finely grated **garlic**

1 To make the dressing, combine the rice wine vinegar, sugar, sesame oil, soy sauce, ginger, and garlic in a small bowl. Whisk until the sugar has dissolved.

2 Place the zucchini, cucumber, sprouted mung beans, pea shoots, red onion, and mint in a serving bowl. Pour the dressing over the top and toss until the salad is well coated, piling the salad into the middle of the bowl.

3 Sprinkle with the chopped peanuts and a few extra mint leaves (if using) and serve immediately.

the good stuff

Sprouted mung beans may be little, but they fill you up. They are also a great source of protein. Sprouted beans can carry harmful bacteria, so children, the elderly, pregnant women, and those with weakened immune systems should avoid eating them raw.

flex it

A few thinly cut strips of
grilled chicken make a lovely
addition to this salad for
meat-eaters.

WARM HARISSA SALAD
with sorghum & chickpeas

SERVES 4
PREP 5 MINS
COOK 1 HR

1 cup **sorghum**
2 **red bell peppers**, seeded and
    cut into bite-sized pieces
2 **red onions**, diced
1 tbsp **light olive oil**
2 x 14oz (400g) cans
    chickpeas, drained
1 tbsp **harissa paste**
juice of 1 **lemon**
salt and freshly ground
    black pepper
5 cups **arugula leaves**
4 tbsp roughly chopped
    flat-leaf parsley, to garnish

1 Rinse the sorghum under running water and place in a large, lidded saucepan. Cover with water and bring to a boil. Reduce the heat to a simmer and cook, covered, for 50–60 minutes, until tender. Drain the sorghum and put into a large bowl.

2 Meanwhile, preheat the oven to 400°F (200°C). Place the red bell peppers and onions on a baking sheet, drizzle with the olive oil, and toss to coat. Bake in the oven for 30–40 minutes, until softened. Add the peppers and onions to the sorghum and mix well.

3 Add the chickpeas and harissa paste to the sorghum mixture. Toss to combine, so the vegetables and chickpeas are evenly coated. Pour over the lemon juice and season to taste. Divide the arugula among 4 plates and top with the sorghum salad. Garnish with parsley and serve immediately.

the good stuff

Sorghum is high in fiber and gluten-free, so it is a great alternative grain. It also contains vitamins such as niacin, riboflavin, and thiamine.

FREEKEH & CORN SALAD
with kale & zucchini

SERVES 4–6
PREP 20 MINS, plus cooling
COOK 30 MINS

1 cup **freekeh**

2 cups **vegetable stock**

2 **corn on the cob**

1 tbsp **olive oil**

¾ cup **almonds**,
  roughly chopped

3 tbsp **sesame seeds**

10–12 **kale leaves**, ribs removed
  and finely chopped

1 × 15oz (425g) can **chickpeas**

4–6 **scallions**, chopped

1 green **zucchini**, diced

1 yellow **zucchini**, diced

TAHINI DRESSING

3 tbsp **tahini**

1 **garlic clove**, pressed

2 tbsp **lemon juice**

1 tsp **low-sodium soy sauce**

1 tsp **toasted sesame oil**

salt and freshly ground
  black pepper

1 Rinse the freekeh under cold running water, drain well, and place in a lidded saucepan. Add the vegetable stock and bring to a boil. Then reduce the heat to a simmer, cover, and cook for about 20 minutes. Remove from the heat and leave to stand, covered, for 5 minutes. Uncover and leave to cool completely.

2 Bring a large pan of water to a boil. Add the corn and cook for 10 minutes or until the corn kernels are tender. Remove from the pan and rinse under cold running water. Remove the kernels from the cob by slicing down lengthwise with a knife.

3 For the tahini dressing, place the tahini, garlic, lemon juice, soy sauce, and sesame oil in a small bowl. Add 2 tablespoons of water, and whisk until well combined. Taste, adjusting the seasoning if necessary, and set aside.

4 Heat the olive oil in a small nonstick frying pan over low heat. Add the almonds and sesame seeds and toast for 2–3 minutes or until the almonds are lightly browned. Remove from the heat and leave to cool.

5 Place the kale in a large bowl and drizzle with some of the dressing. Toss well to coat. Then add the corn, almonds, sesame seeds, chickpeas, scallions, and green and yellow zucchini. Drizzle over more of the seasoning and toss well to coat. Add the freekeh and the remaining seasoning and mix well to combine. Serve immediately.

GAZPACHO SALAD
with hot sauce dressing

SERVES 2
PREP 15 MINS
COOK 15 MINS

2 **tomatoes**, quartered
1 tsp **olive oil**
pinch of **ground cinnamon**
pinch of **chili flakes**
sea salt and freshly ground
   black pepper
½ cup cooked **beets**,
   roughly chopped
⅔ cup **cucumber**, sliced
¼ **red bell pepper**, roughly
   chopped
¼ **green bell pepper**, roughly
   chopped
1 **celery stick**, sliced
1 **garlic clove**, grated
1 **scallion**, green part only,
   finely sliced
½ **avocado**
juice of 1 **lemon**
a few **basil leaves**

DRESSING
1 tsp **extra virgin olive oil**
a few drops of **hot sauce**

1 Preheat the oven to 400°F (200°C). Mix the tomatoes, olive oil, cinnamon, and chili flakes in a roasting pan, and season with sea salt and pepper. Roast for 10–15 minutes, or until the tomatoes start to split. Set aside.

2 Mix the beets, cucumber, red bell pepper, green bell pepper, celery, garlic, and scallion in a bowl.

3 Make the dressing by mixing the olive oil and hot sauce in a bowl, then toss it through the vegetables, add the roasted tomatoes, and toss again.

4 Chop the avocado roughly, then toss with the lemon juice to prevent discoloration.

5 Spoon the gazpacho salad into a serving bowl, then add the avocado and sprinkle over the basil leaves.

the good stuff

This is a generous serving of vegetables in one bowl. Packed with goodness, the avocado provides a substantial amount of your daily monounsaturated fatty acids.

flex it

Delicate fresh crab meat
makes a delicious addition
to this salad for nonvegans.
Just scatter it over
the relevant bowls.

flex it

If your meat-eaters need a little something extra, drape a few anchovy fillets over the salad just before serving for a salty kick.

LIMA BEAN PANZANELLA
with sourdough chunks

SERVES 6
PREP 25 MINS
COOK 15 MINS

1 small loaf **sourdough bread**
1⅛ cups **cherry tomatoes**, halved
1¼ cups **cooked lima beans**
1 **cucumber**, diced
1 cup fresh **sweetcorn kernels**
salt and freshly ground **black pepper**

DRESSING
¼ cup **red wine vinegar**
1 tbsp **Dijon mustard**
½ cup **olive oil**
2 **garlic cloves**, finely chopped
1 tsp chopped **oregano**
1 tsp chopped **basil leaves**

1 Preheat the oven to 325°F (170°C). Cut the bread into ½in (1cm) cubes. On a baking sheet, arrange the bread cubes in a single layer and bake for 15 minutes, or until toasted and light golden brown.

2 Meanwhile, to make the dressing, in a small bowl whisk together the red wine vinegar and Dijon mustard. While whisking, drizzle in the olive oil and thoroughly combine. Stir in the garlic, oregano, and basil. Set aside.

3 To assemble, in a large salad bowl, add the tomatoes, lima beans, cucumber, and sweetcorn. Fold in the toasted bread, then drizzle the dressing over. Toss to coat. Season with salt and pepper to taste. Serve immediately.

the good stuff

Sourdough is more digestible than standard bread, and the lactic acids make the nutrients in the flour easier for your body to absorb. Lima beans, with their high levels of B vitamins, are a must for the vegan pantry.

HERBED ZUCCHINI
with tangy lemon zest

SERVES 4
PREP 10 MINS
COOK 20 MINS

2 large **zucchini**

4 tbsp **plant-based mayonnaise**

3¼ cups **panko breadcrumbs**

8 tbsp finely chopped fresh mixed
   herbs, such as **parsley**, **chives**,
   chervil, and/or **tarragon**

½ cup **extra virgin olive oil**

2 tsp **sea salt**

1 tsp freshly ground **black pepper**

2 tsp **lemon zest**

1 Preheat the oven to 400°F (200°C). Line a baking sheet with parchment paper.

2 Trim each zucchini, cut into ¼in (5mm) slices. Blot dry with paper towel and brush both sides of each zucchini slice with plant-based mayonnaise.

3 In a small, shallow bowl, combine the panko breadcrumbs, herbs, olive oil, sea salt, black pepper, and lemon zest.

4 Dredge each zucchini slice in the panko mixture, coating both sides, and lay the slices on the prepared baking sheet.

5 Bake for 20 minutes, carefully turning with a spatula halfway through cooking, and serve immediately.

the good stuff

Fresh herbs are really good for you—as well as adding tons of flavor to plant-based dishes, they contain flavonoids and have mild anti-inflammatory properties.

flex it

For an extra flavor kick, make a few zucchini pieces for nonvegans with some chopped anchovies in the panko mix.

flex it

If you want to make it "meatier," grill 4oz (100g) shrimp and scatter them over the dish before serving.

ROASTED TOMATOES & WHITE BEANS
with basil vinaigrette

SERVES 4
PREP 15 MINS
COOK 30 MINS

4 **plum tomatoes**
2 **garlic cloves**, finely chopped
1 tbsp **olive oil**
1¼ cups cooked **cannellini**
  or **flageolet beans**

BASIL VINAIGRETTE
¾ cup **basil leaves**,
  plus extra to garnish
¼ cup **white wine** or
  champagne vinegar
2 tbsp **olive oil**
salt and freshly ground
  black pepper

1 Preheat the oven to 400°F (200°C). Cut the plum tomatoes in half lengthwise and toss with the garlic and the olive oil. Arrange on a baking sheet and roast for 30 minutes. Let cool to room temperature.

2 Meanwhile, to make the basil vinaigrette, in a blender or food processor, add the basil and vinegar. With the processor running on low, drizzle in the 2 tablespoons of olive oil until emulsified. Season with salt and pepper to taste.

3 In a mixing bowl, toss the beans with 2 tablespoons of dressing and spread on a serving plate. Arrange the roasted tomatoes on top. Season with salt and pepper. Garnish with any remaining dressing and basil leaves. Serve immediately.

the good stuff

As well as being packed with vitamins, tomatoes are also high in heart-healthy lycopene. Cooking tomatoes with a little oil makes it easier for your body to absorb this powerful nutrient.

GRILLED VEGETABLES
with garlic & parsley

SERVES 4
PREP 20 MINS,
  plus marinating
COOK 10 MINS

2 **zucchini**, halved
  lengthwise
1 large **red bell pepper,**
  quartered lengthwise
  and seeded
1 large **yellow bell**
  pepper, quartered
  lengthwise and seeded
1 large **eggplant**, sliced
1 **fennel bulb**, quartered
  lengthwise
½ cup **olive oil,** plus extra
  for brushing
3 tbsp **balsamic vinegar**
2 **garlic cloves**, chopped
4 tbsp coarsely chopped
  flat-leaf parsley, plus
  extra to serve
salt and freshly ground
  black pepper

1 Arrange the vegetables, cut-side up, in a large nonmetallic dish. Whisk together the olive oil, vinegar, garlic and parsley, and season to taste with salt and pepper. Spoon over the vegetables and leave to marinate for at least 30 minutes.

2 Light the grill or preheat the oven on its highest setting. Grease the grill rack.

3 Lift the vegetables out of the marinade and place them on the grill or under the broiler for 3–5 minutes on each side, or until tender and lightly charred, brushing with any extra marinade. Serve sprinkled with parsley, with any remaining marinade spooned over.

SPICED CHICKPEAS
with spinach

SERVES 4
PREP 10 MINS
COOK 10 MINS

3 tbsp **olive oil**
1 thick slice of **crusty**
  white bread, torn
  into chunks
1lb 10oz (750g) **spinach**
  leaves
1½ cups **cooked**
  chickpeas
2 **garlic cloves**, finely
  chopped
salt and freshly ground
  black pepper
1 tsp **paprika**
1 tsp **ground cumin**
1 tbsp **sherry vinegar**

1 Heat 1 tablespoon of the olive oil in a frying pan and fry the bread, stirring, until crisp. Remove from the pan, drain on paper towel, and reserve.

2 Rinse the spinach and shake off any excess water. Place it in a large saucepan and cook over low heat, tossing constantly so it does not stick to the pan. When it has wilted, transfer the spinach to a colander and squeeze out as much water as possible by pressing it with a wooden spoon, then place on a chopping board and chop coarsely.

3 Heat the remaining oil in the frying pan, add the spinach, and allow it to warm through before stirring in the chickpeas and garlic. Season to taste with salt and pepper. Add the paprika and cumin, then crumble in the reserved fried bread.

4 Add the vinegar and 2 tablespoons of water and allow to heat through for several minutes. Divide among 4 small plates and serve immediately.

PATATAS BRAVAS
with lemon & garlic

SERVES 4
PREP 15 MINS
COOK 1 HR 10 MINS

6 tbsp **olive oil**
1½lb (700g) **white potatoes**,
    peeled and cut into ¾in
    (2cm) cubes
2 **onions**, finely chopped
1 tsp **dried chili flakes**
2 tbsp **dry sherry (vegan)**
grated zest of 1 **lemon**
4 **garlic cloves**, grated or
    finely chopped
1 × 7oz (200g) can **chopped
    tomatoes**
small handful of **flat-leaf
    parsley**, chopped
salt and freshly ground
    black pepper

1 Preheat the oven to 400°F (200°C). Heat half the olive oil in a nonstick frying pan, add the potatoes, and cook over low heat for 20 minutes, or until starting to brown, turning frequently. Add the onions and cook for another 5 minutes.

2 Add the chili flakes, sherry, lemon zest, and garlic. Reduce for 2 minutes before adding the tomatoes and parsley. Season, combine well, and cook over medium heat for 10 minutes, stirring occasionally.

3 Stir in the remaining oil, place all the ingredients in a shallow baking dish, and bake in the oven for 30 minutes, or until cooked. Serve hot with a selection of tapas dishes.

flex it

Keep die-hard meat-eaters happy by frying some slices of chorizo with a separate portion of potatoes, then add the flavorings and tomatoes.

PEPERONATA
with tomatoes & basil

SERVES 4
PREP 10 MINS
COOK 40 MINS

2 tbsp **olive oil**
1 mild **onion**, finely sliced
1 **garlic clove**, crushed (optional)
2 large **red bell peppers** or 1 **red**
   and 1 **yellow bell pepper**, halved,
   cored, seeded, and cut into strips
salt and freshly ground
   black pepper
4 ripe **tomatoes**, chopped
a few **basil leaves**, rolled
   and snipped

1 Pour the olive oil into a nonstick frying pan over medium heat. Stir in the onion and cook for 5–8 minutes, until soft stirring frequently. Add the garlic, if using, then stir in the bell peppers, season, and soften for 5 minutes, stirring often.

2 Add the tomatoes, stir well, and partially cover the pan. Cook for 20–30 minutes until just soft but not too mushy, stirring occasionally. Season to taste and stir in the basil. Serve warm or at room temperature.

VARIATION

For a tasty combination, add a chopped eggplant to the pan with the peppers. You could also stir in some cooked chopped potato.

the good stuff

Bell peppers add a healthy boost to your meal, as they are loaded with vitamins, especially C— just half a cup has almost double your daily needs.

CASSEROLES & ONE POTS

flex it

Serve with a bowl of
grated Parmesan cheese
for nonvegans to
sprinkle liberally over
their portions.

IMAM BAYILDI
(Turkish stuffed eggplant)

SERVES 6
PREP 15 MINS, plus soaking
COOK 1 HR 10 MINS

6 small **eggplants**
½ cup **extra virgin olive oil**, plus
  extra to taste
3 large **sweet onions**, halved and
  thinly sliced
6 ripe **plum tomatoes**, peeled,
  julienned, and juice reserved
6 **garlic cloves**, thinly sliced
4 tbsp **flat-leaf parsley**, finely
  chopped, plus extra to garnish
¼ cup **pine nuts**, toasted
  (optional)

1 Fill the kitchen sink or a large bowl with well-salted water. Cut a small slit in each eggplant, remove the stems (if desired), transfer them to the salt-water bath, and soak for 1 hour. Drain, squeeze gently, and pat dry.

2 Heat the olive oil in a wide, heat-resistant frying pan or a cast-iron casserole dish with a lid over medium heat. Add the onions and cook, stirring occasionally, for 5–10 minutes or until golden.

3 Add the eggplants, plum tomatoes, and garlic; reduce the heat to medium-low (adjust as needed); cover; and cook, stirring the onions once or twice without disturbing the eggplants, for 10 minutes.

4 Turn over the eggplants and cook for another 10 minutes.

5 Preheat the oven to 375°F (190°C).

6 Remove the pan from the heat and gently stuff some onion–tomato mixture into each eggplant. Pour the reserved tomato juice over the eggplants, sprinkle with flat-leaf parsley, cover tightly with a lid or aluminum foil, and bake for 35–40 minutes.

7 Remove from the oven and cool slightly before garnishing with toasted pine nuts (if using) and serving.

the good stuff

You can get your vital B vitamins from eggplants. Be sure to eat the skin, too, as this where all those health-boosting antioxidants are concentrated.

WINTER VEGETABLE PIE
with potato & fava beans

SERVES 6
PREP 15 MINS
COOK 45 MINS

4 tbsp **grapeseed oil**
3 tbsp **all-purpose flour**
3 cups **vegetable stock**
1 large **onion**, cut into small dice
4 large **celery sticks**, cut into small dice
3 **carrots**, cut into small dice
4¼ cups **chestnut mushrooms**, quartered
3 **garlic cloves**, minced
4 large **red-skinned potatoes**, cut into small dice
1 **sweet potato**, cut into small dice
2½ cups **frozen fava beans**
1 **bay leaf**
1 tsp **dried thyme**
1 tsp **sea salt**, plus extra to taste
½ tsp freshly ground **black pepper**
1 sheet **vegan puff** or **shortcrust pastry**, thawed

1 Preheat the oven to 400°F (200°C). Heat 2 tablespoons of the grapeseed oil in a small saucepan over medium heat. Whisk in the flour until smooth, and cook, stirring constantly, for about 2 minutes or until the flour is lightly golden and smells toasty.

2 Whisk in 2 cups of the vegetable stock, and simmer for 5 minutes. Remove from the heat and set aside.

3 Heat the remaining oil in a wide frying pan over medium-high heat. Add the onion, celery, carrots, mushrooms, and garlic, and cook, stirring frequently, for about 10 minutes, or until the vegetables are softened and beginning to color.

4 Stir in the remaining stock, potatoes, sweet potatoes, fava beans, bay leaf, thyme, sea salt, and black pepper. Cover and cook, stirring once or twice and adding a bit of water if it seems dry, for 10 minutes.

5 Remove the bay leaf, stir in the reserved sauce, and pour the vegetable mixture into a 9 × 13in (23 × 33cm) baking dish.

6 Roll out the pastry on a floured surface to fit the top of the baking dish with an overhang of ½in (1cm). Prick all over with a fork, transfer it to the baking dish, and lay it gently over the vegetables. Tuck the overhanging edge down into the inside of the dish.

7 Bake for about 30 minutes or until the pastry is puffed and the filling is hot and bubbling. Serve immediately.

the good stuff

Comfort food can be nutritious—this pie is full of healthy root vegetables and fava beans, which are stuffed with protein and energy-giving folate, as well as B vitamins.

flex it

Add chunky pieces of cooked chicken to a few portions of the mix before topping with pastry, or use a butter pastry if not following a vegan diet.

flex it

For the meat-eaters in the house, add 10oz (300g) of cooked ground beef to the vegetable mix before filling the tortillas.

VEGETABLE ENCHILADAS
with roasted tomato sauce

SERVES 4
PREP 20 MINS
COOK 1 HR 40 MINS

4 tbsp **extra virgin olive oil**

1¼ lb (550g) **small tomatoes**, such as Campari, cut in half

2 **red bell peppers**, seeded and cut into 1in (2.5cm) strips

1 tsp **sea salt**

½ tsp **dried oregano**

2 cups **vegetable stock**

3 tbsp **chili powder**

1 large **onion**, finely chopped

2 **poblano chile peppers**, seeded and finely chopped

2 **garlic cloves**, finely chopped

2 large **zucchini**, cut into ½in (1cm) dice

1lb (450g) **roasted sweetcorn kernels** or regular **frozen sweetcorn kernels**

1 x 14oz (400g) can **black beans**, rinsed and drained

2 tbsp finely chopped **cilantro leaves**

16 x 6in (15cm) **tortillas**

½ cup shredded **plant-based Cheddar–style cheese** (optional)

1 Preheat the oven to 375°F (190°C). Lightly coat a 9 × 13in (23 × 33cm) baking dish with a little of the olive oil. Place the tomatoes in the baking dish and toss with 2 tablespoons of the olive oil, red bell pepper strips, ½ teaspoon of the sea salt, and oregano. Roast for 1 hour, stirring occasionally, and cool slightly.

2 Purée the tomato mixture, vegetable stock, and chili powder in batches in a blender or a food processor. Set aside.

3 Heat the remaining oil in a wide frying pan over medium-high heat. Add the onion and poblano chiles, and cook, stirring occasionally, for 4–5 minutes, adjusting the heat as necessary. Add the garlic and stir for 1 minute. Add the zucchini and cook for 4–5 minutes or until the vegetables are golden. Stir in the corn and cook for 1 or 2 minutes. Stir in the black beans, cilantro, remaining sea salt, and ½ cup of the reserved sauce. Remove from the heat.

4 Spread ½ cup of the sauce on the bottom of the dish. Spoon about one-twelfth of the filling into the center of 1 tortilla, filling it generously. Roll, then set in the dish. Repeat with the remaining tortillas and filling, fitting them in snugly. Pour over the remaining sauce, lightly covering the enchiladas with the edges exposed, and sprinkle with cheese (if using). Cover with aluminum foil and bake for about 40 minutes or until hot and bubbling. Serve immediately.

the good stuff

If you can handle the heat, hot chiles are beneficial for health; the capsaicin they contain is thought to have powerful anti-cancer properties.

HEARTY CHILI
with mixed beans

SERVES 6
PREP 10 MINS
COOK 1 HR

4 tbsp **extra virgin olive oil**

2 large **onions**, diced

4 **red bell peppers**, seeded
and diced

2 **yellow bell peppers**, seeded
and diced

4¼ cups **chestnut mushrooms**,
thinly sliced

4 **garlic cloves**, finely chopped

1 tsp **sea salt**

2 tbsp **chili powder**

1 tsp **ground cumin**

1 tsp **Anaheim chili powder**

1 tsp **dried oregano**

1 tsp freshly ground **black pepper**

4 x 14oz (400g) cans **chopped
tomatoes**, with juice

2 x 14oz (400g) cans **kidney beans**,
rinsed and drained

2 x 14oz (400g) cans **black beans**,
rinsed and drained

1 tbsp **habanero hot pepper
sauce**, plus extra to serve

plant-based sour cream
(optional), to serve

tortilla chips (optional), to serve

1 Heat the olive oil in a large, deep-sided pan or stockpot over
medium heat. Add the onions and red and yellow bell peppers,
and cook, stirring often, for 10 minutes.

2 Stir in the chestnut mushrooms, garlic, sea salt, chili powder,
cumin, Anaheim chili powder, oregano, and black pepper, and
cook, stirring frequently, for 10 minutes.

3 Add the chopped tomatoes, stir, and bring to a boil. Reduce the
heat to low or medium-low and cook at a gently bubbling simmer,
uncovered, for about 30 minutes or until the peppers and onions are
very tender.

4 Stir in the kidney beans, black beans, and hot pepper sauce, and
cook for 5 minutes. Serve in big bowls with a spoonful of plant-
based sour cream (if using) and plenty of tortilla chips (if using).

the good stuff

When eating a plant-based diet, try to introduce
beans daily, because they contain important
macro- and micronutrients, such as protein, iron,
zinc, folate, fiber, and potassium. They also
promote the growth of beneficial gut bacteria.

flex it

Chili is a great dish for batch-cooking and keeping in the freezer for a speedy dinner. Add some cooked ground beef or stewing beef to a few portions for meat-eaters.

MOROCCAN SQUASH TAGINE
with pigeon peas

SERVES 6
PREP 45 MINS
COOK 40 MINS

1 tbsp **coconut oil**
1 **onion**, chopped
1 **carrot**, diced
2 **garlic cloves**, finely chopped
1 tsp grated **fresh ginger**
1 tsp **smoked paprika**
1 **cinnamon stick**
¼ tsp **allspice**
½ tsp **ground coriander**
¼ tsp **ground cardamom**
2 tbsp **tomato paste**
2 cups **vegetable stock**
1 large **acorn** or **butternut squash**,
   peeled, seeded, and diced, about
   1½lb (675g)
2 cups cooked **pigeon peas**
juice of 1 large **lemon**
½ cup **dates**, pitted
   and chopped
salt and freshly ground
   black pepper

1 In a tagine pot or large heat-resistant casserole dish, heat the coconut oil over medium-low heat. Add the onion and carrot and cook for 2–3 minutes. Add the garlic and ginger and cook, uncovered, for an additional 1–2 minutes.

2 Add the smoked paprika, cinnamon stick, allspice, coriander, and cardamom. Cook for 1 minute to warm the spices. Add the tomato paste and vegetable stock, and stir to combine.

3 Stir in the squash and simmer, covered, for 15 minutes. Add the pigeon peas and cook for an additional 10 minutes, or until the squash is tender and the peas are warmed through. Stir in the lemon juice and dates. Season with salt and pepper to taste. Remove the cinnamon stick and serve immediately.

the good stuff

Dates contain B6 and magnesium, and they make a great energy-boosting snack. However, they are also high in sugar, so only eat them in small amounts.

BLACK-EYED PEA & COCONUT CASSEROLE
with garlic & ginger

SERVES 4
PREP 15 MINS
COOK 45 MINS

1 tbsp **olive oil**

1 **onion**, finely chopped

2 **garlic cloves**, finely chopped

1 x 2in (5cm) piece of **fresh ginger**, peeled and finely chopped

1 **bay leaf**

1 tsp **coriander seeds**, crushed

2 x 14oz (400g) cans **black-eyed peas**, drained and rinsed

1 x 14oz (400g) can **coconut milk**

2½ cups **vegetable stock**

3 **potatoes**, peeled and cut into bite-sized pieces

salt and freshly ground **black pepper**

1⅛ cups **basmati rice**

1 Heat the olive oil in a large pan, add the onion, and cook until soft. Stir in the garlic, ginger, bay leaf, and coriander seeds, and cook for a couple of minutes, being careful not to burn the garlic.

2 Stir in the black-eyed peas, then add the coconut milk and vegetable stock and bring to a boil. Reduce the heat and simmer, partially covered, for about 15 minutes. Add the potatoes and cook for another 10 minutes or until they are done. If the casserole needs more liquid, top up with stock, but don't let it become runny. Taste and season as needed, and remove the bay leaf.

3 Meanwhile, put the basmati rice in a large pan, cover with water, and cook for 10–15 minutes or according to the package instructions. Once the rice is cooked, remove it from the heat, cover the pan, and leave it to steam for a few more minutes. Either add the rice to the casserole or serve it separately.

flex it

If you want to add some meat to this dish, brown about 4½oz (125g) pork and add it to the baking dish with the bean mix.

KIDNEY BEAN CASSOULET
with thyme & chiles

SERVES 4
PREP 20 MINS
COOK 45 MINS

2 tbsp **olive oil**
1 small **onion**, diced
1 **carrot**, diced
1 **celery stick**, diced
2 **garlic cloves**, finely chopped
3 sprigs of **thyme**
1 **bay leaf**
pinch of **crushed dried chiles**
1⅔ cups cooked **kidney beans**
⅔ cup **tomato purée**
¾ cup **vegetable stock**
salt and freshly ground
   black pepper
¾ cup **panko breadcrumbs**
1 tbsp chopped **flat-leaf parsley**

1 Preheat the oven to 400°F (200°C). Lightly oil an 8-cup baking dish with olive oil.

2 In a stockpot or heat-resistant casserole dish, heat the olive oil over medium-low heat. Add the onion, carrot, and celery, and cook for 2–3 minutes until soft. Add the garlic and cook for an additional minute.

3 Incorporate the thyme, bay leaf, chiles, kidney beans, tomato purée, and vegetable stock. Simmer, covered, for 20 minutes.

4 Remove the bay leaf and thyme sprigs. In a blender or food processor, purée about ½ cup of the bean mixture until smooth. Return the puréed mixture to the pot and stir to combine. Season with salt and pepper to taste. Transfer the bean mixture to the baking dish.

5 To make the topping, in a small bowl, combine the breadcrumbs and parsley. Top the dish evenly with the breadcrumb mixture. Bake for 20 minutes, or until golden brown. Serve immediately.

the good stuff

Kidney beans offer many of the key nutritional elements that are essential in a vegan diet; they are high in protein and fiber, and also provide potassium, phosphorus, iron, and thiamine.

POLENTA LASAGNA
with eggplant & roasted tomatoes

SERVES 6
PREP 45 MINS, plus chilling
COOK 1 HR 10 MINS

4 tbsp **extra virgin olive oil**

1 cup **coarse polenta**
  (not instant)

1½ tsp **sea salt**

1 large **eggplant**, cut into 1in
  (2.5cm) cubes

2⅓ cups **cherry tomatoes**,
  halved

3 **garlic cloves**, thinly sliced

1½ cups homemade or store-
  bought **tomato sauce**

1 cup **dairy-free pesto**

6 large **basil leaves**, cut into
  thin ribbons

½ cup **pine nuts**, toasted

the good stuff

Polenta is a cooked cornmeal that contains protein and fiber to help you feel full. The pine nuts are a good source of magnesium, which may help boost energy and fight fatigue.

1 Line a 9 × 9in (23 × 23cm) baking dish with parchment paper and brush it with a little olive oil. In a large saucepan over high heat, bring 4 cups of water to a boil. Stirring constantly, add the polenta in a thin stream. Add ½ teaspoon of the sea salt, reduce the heat to medium, and stir until the polenta is fully cooked. (It will be creamy and smooth with no "bite.") Pour into the prepared baking dish and allow to cool. Cover and refrigerate for at least 2 hours or overnight until set.

2 Preheat the oven to 400°F (200°C). Sprinkle the eggplant cubes with ½ teaspoon of the sea salt and drain in a colander for 30 minutes. Rinse and gently squeeze out any water.

3 In a large baking sheet, toss the eggplant and cherry tomatoes with garlic and 3 tablespoons of the olive oil. Spread evenly, and roast, stirring once or twice, for 30 minutes. Remove from the oven, and reduce the temperature to 375°F (190°C). When the polenta has set, carefully turn it out, cut into thirds, and slice each third horizontally into 3 equal pieces so you have 9 polenta "lasagna sheets." Handle carefully using a spatula—if they break, fit them together in the dish.

4 To assemble the lasagna, brush the baking dish with the remaining olive oil. Spread ½ cup of tomato sauce over the bottom and cover with 3 pieces of polenta. Top with half of the tomato–eggplant mixture and half of the pesto, followed by another polenta layer. Add another ½ cup of tomato sauce, the remaining eggplant–tomato mixture, and the remaining pesto. Top with the final layer of polenta and spread the remaining tomato sauce evenly on top. Cover and bake for about 40 minutes or until hot and bubbling.

5 Just before serving, sprinkle the basil and toasted pine nuts over the top of the lasagna. Serve hot.

MUSHROOM LASAGNA
with shiitake & porcini mushrooms

SERVES 8
PREP 30 MINS
COOK 1 HR 5 MINS

2 tbsp **dried porcini mushrooms**

4 tbsp **extra virgin olive oil**

3 **garlic cloves**, minced

3¼ cups **chestnut mushrooms**, thinly sliced

¾ cup **shiitake mushrooms**, stemmed and thinly sliced

1 tsp chopped **rosemary** or ½ tsp dried

1 tsp **sea salt**, or to taste

½ tsp **dried oregano**

½ tsp freshly ground **black pepper**, or to taste

4 tbsp **dry red wine**

3¾ cups homemade or store-bought **tomato sauce**

9 ready-to-use **egg-free lasagna sheets**

2 cups **Cashew Ricotta** (see p.66)

1. Preheat the oven to 375°F (190°C). Lightly coat a 9 × 13in (23 × 33cm) baking dish with cooking spray.

2. Place the porcini mushrooms in a small bowl, pour over ½ cup of boiling water, and soak for about 5 minutes or until softened. Lift the porcini from the water, agitating gently to release any soil. Reserve the soaking liquid. Chop the porcini and set aside.

3. Heat the olive oil in a large frying pan over medium-high heat. Add the garlic and cook, stirring continuously, for 1 minute.

4. Add the porcini, keeping the liquid, the shiitake mushrooms, rosemary, sea salt, oregano, and black pepper, and cook, stirring occasionally, for 10 minutes or until the mushrooms begin to brown.

5. Strain the mushroom liquid, leaving a few teaspoons behind to eliminate grit, and add to the mushrooms with the red wine, stirring vigorously to deglaze the pan. Stir until the liquid has evaporated, and set the mushrooms aside.

6. Spread 1 cup of tomato sauce evenly over the bottom of the baking dish, lay 3 sheets of lasagna over the sauce, spoon half of the mushroom mixture and half of the Cashew Ricotta evenly over the lasagna sheets. Pour ¾ cup of tomato sauce over the Cashew Ricotta, layer another 3 lasagna sheets, add the remaining mushrooms and Cashew Ricotta, followed by another ¾ cup of tomato sauce. Finish with 3 lasagna sheets and another ¾ cup of tomato sauce. Cover with aluminum foil, folding back a corner slightly to allow steam to escape. Reserve the remaining ½ cup of sauce to serve.

7. Bake for 50 minutes or until bubbling. Set aside for 5–10 minutes before cutting. Reheat the remaining sauce before serving.

SQUASH & ONION BAKE
with nutmeg & rosemary

SERVES 4
PREP 15 MINS
COOK 45 MINS

4 tbsp **extra virgin olive oil**
2 large **sweet onions**, thinly sliced
   into rings
2 **garlic cloves**, finely chopped
2 **zucchini**, thinly sliced
2 **yellow squash**, thinly sliced
1 tsp **sea salt**
¼ tsp freshly ground **black pepper**
2 tbsp **all-purpose flour**
1½ cups **nondairy milk**, such as
   rice or **soy milk**
¼ tsp **ground nutmeg**
½ tsp finely chopped **rosemary**
2 cups **panko breadcrumbs**
2 tbsp finely chopped **chives**
1 tsp **dried thyme**

flex it

For a meaty version, cook 10oz (300g) of ground beef or pork with the onions, and assemble and bake as per the recipe.

1 Preheat the oven to 350°F (180°C). Lightly grease a 8 × 8in (20 x 20cm) square baking dish.

2 Heat 2 tablespoons of the olive oil in a wide frying pan over medium-high heat. Add the sweet onions and cook, stirring, for 5 minutes or until softened.

3 Add the garlic and stir for 1 minute. Remove the onions and garlic from the pan and keep warm.

4 Add 1 tablespoon of the olive oil, zucchini, and yellow squash, and season with sea salt and black pepper. Increase the heat to high and cook, stirring every minute or so, for 5 minutes or until the vegetables begin to turn golden.

5 Sprinkle with the flour, reduce the heat to medium, and stir for 1 minute to combine well. Return the onion mixture to the pan.

6 Stir in the nondairy milk, nutmeg, and rosemary. Bring to a boil, and cook for about 2 minutes or until thickened.

7 In a small bowl, combine the panko breadcrumbs, chives, thyme, and the remaining olive oil.

8 Gently spread the squash mixture in the baking dish, and sprinkle evenly with the breadcrumbs. Bake, uncovered, for 30 minutes. Serve immediately.

flex it

This works really well with meat, too—just cook some ground lamb and combine it with an equal amount of lentils before topping and baking.

SPICED SWEET POTATO SHEPHERD'S PIE
with cumin & turmeric

SERVES 6
PREP 35 MINS
COOK 50 MINS

3 **sweet potatoes**, peeled and diced

⅓ cup **plant-based cream**

salt and freshly ground **black pepper**

1 tbsp **olive oil**

1 **onion**, chopped

1 **garlic clove**, finely chopped

1lb 2oz (500g) cooked **brown lentils**

1 tbsp **ground cumin**

1 tbsp **garam masala**

2 tsp **curry powder**

1 tsp **ground turmeric**

1¾ cups **vegetable stock**

1 cup chopped **cilantro leaves**

¾ cup **panko breadcrumbs**

1 Preheat the oven to 375°F (190°C). In a large saucepan, bring 5 cups of water to a boil. Cook the potatoes for 15–20 minutes until tender. Drain thoroughly and transfer to a large mixing bowl. With a potato masher, mash the potatoes and plant-based cream until smooth. Season with salt and pepper to taste.

2 Meanwhile, in a large frying pan, warm the olive oil over medium heat. Add the onion and cook for 2 minutes, or until soft. Add the garlic and cook for an additional minute.

3 Add the lentils, cumin, garam masala, curry powder, and turmeric. Stir to combine and cook for 1–2 minutes to warm the spices. Add the vegetable stock and cook for 5 minutes. Stir in the chopped cilantro.

4 Pour the lentil mixture evenly into a 9 x 12in (23 × 30cm) glass or ceramic baking dish. Top with the mashed sweet potato. Bake for 15 minutes. Sprinkle evenly with the panko breadcrumbs and bake for another 10 minutes, or until lightly browned. Cool for 10 minutes before serving.

the good stuff

Everyone can benefit from including nutritional lentils in their diet—they will give you slow, steady energy, and are also a quick-cooking and tasty plant-based protein.

DESSERTS

flex it

Serve some dairy custard
or cream in a pitcher
alongside the crumble
for nonvegans.

ROASTED STONE FRUIT
with millet crumble

SERVES 4
PREP 15 MINS, plus cooling
COOK 1 HR

FRUIT FILLING
1¾lb (800g) **mixed fruit**, such as
  peaches, nectarines, and **plums,**
  pitted and roughly chopped
1 tbsp **coconut oil,**
  room temperature

CRUMBLE TOPPING
½ cup **millet flakes**
1 cup **ground almonds**
¼ cup **coconut oil,**
  chilled and diced
½ cup **unrefined powdered sugar**

plant-based cream, to serve

1 Preheat the oven to 400°F (200°C). For the filling, place the fruit in a roasting pan, drizzle over the coconut oil, and toss to coat. Roast in the oven for 20–30 minutes, until tender but still holding their shape. Remove from the oven and leave to cool for at least 10 minutes.

2 For the crumble topping, place the millet flakes and almonds in a bowl and mix well to combine. Rub in the coconut oil and mix well until the mixture resembles rough breadcrumbs. Add the powdered sugar and gently stir to combine.

3 Place the cooled fruit mixture in an 8 x 10in (20 x 25cm) shallow baking dish and spread it out in an even layer. Sprinkle the topping evenly over the fruit. Place in the oven and bake for 20–30 minutes, until the topping is golden brown. Remove from the heat and serve warm with some plant-based cream.

the good stuff

Stone fruits are low in saturated fat and cholesterol and are a good source of fiber. Topped with healthy millet flakes that are full of magnesium and calcium, this is a good-for-you dessert.

ADZUKI BEAN CHOCOLATE PUDDING
with fresh raspberries

SERVES 6
PREP 10 MINS, plus cooling
  and chilling
COOK 10 MINS

3 tbsp **cornstarch**
2 tbsp plus ⅓ cup **water**
1 cup **cooked adzuki beans**
1 cup **unsweetened**
  almond milk
2 tsp **vanilla bean paste**
¼ cup **agave nectar**
½ cup **vegan unsweetened**
  cocoa powder
6 **raspberries**, to decorate

1 In a small bowl, whisk together the cornstarch and 2 tablespoons of water. Set aside.

2 In a blender, purée the adzuki beans with the remaining ⅓ cup of water and ½ cup of the almond milk until smooth.

3 In a small saucepan, whisk together the remaining ½ cup almond milk, the vanilla bean paste, agave nectar, cocoa powder, and puréed adzuki beans until completely smooth.

4 Heat the almond milk mixture over low heat for 8–10 minutes until the mixture reaches a low simmer, stirring occasionally to avoid lumps. Remove from the heat and let sit at room temperature for 10 minutes.

5 Divide evenly among 6 serving cups, cover, and refrigerate overnight to set. Top each with a raspberry before serving.

the good stuff

This recipe is a clever way to make a chocolate pudding healthy. To really boost the nutritional benefits, use an almond milk that is fortified with calcium.

flex it

For an indulgent extra for nonvegans, serve these with a little scoop of dairy ice cream or whipped cream.

COCONUT & MANGO CHIA PUDDING
with toasted coconut flakes

SERVES 4
PREP 10 MINS, plus chilling

flesh of 1 large **mango**, about
⅔ cup, chopped, plus extra
to serve
1¼ cups **reduced-fat
coconut milk**
3 tbsp **chia seeds**
1 tbsp **maple syrup**
toasted coconut flakes,
to serve (optional)

1 Place the mango and coconut milk in a food processor or blender and blend until smooth.

2 Add the chia seeds and maple syrup and blend briefly to combine. Place the mixture in a bowl, cover, and refrigerate overnight.

3 If the pudding is too thick the next day, thin it with a little coconut milk until it reaches your desired consistency.

4 To serve, top the pudding with chopped fresh mango and toasted coconut flakes.

the good stuff

Mango not only boosts your vitamin C intake, but also helps to keep your eyes healthy, thanks to the antioxidant zeaxanthin. As an added nutritional plus, fiber-packed chia seeds are rich in essential magnesium.

FLOURLESS BLACK BEAN BROWNIES
with vanilla & orange

MAKES 12
PREP 15 MINS
COOK 35 MINS, plus cooling

1 × 14oz (400g) can **black beans**, drained, 9 tbsp of the liquid (aquafaba) reserved

½ cup **agave nectar**

¼ cup **coconut oil**

1 tsp **vanilla extract**

zest of 1 **orange**

¼ tsp **salt**

½ tsp **baking powder**

⅔ cup **powdered sugar**

½ cup **unsweetened cocoa powder**

⅓ cup **vegan dark chocolate chips**

1 Preheat the oven to 350°F (180°C). Lightly oil a 11 x 7in (28 x 18cm) metal baking pan. In a food processor, combine the black beans, agave nectar, coconut oil, vanilla extract, and orange zest until smooth.

2 In a large mixing bowl, combine the salt, baking powder, powdered sugar, and cocoa powder. Incorporate the black bean mixture and aquafaba until well mixed.

3 Gently fold in the dark chocolate chips, being careful not to overwork the mixture.

4 Pour the mixture into the baking pan. Bake for 30–35 minutes, until the brownies pull away from the edge and a skewer inserted into the center comes out clean. Leave to cool for 15–20 minutes before cutting and serving.

the good stuff

Nice but not so naughty—the low glycemic load in beans will help to keep your sugar levels stable, so you won't peak and trough like you would after eating regular brownies.

PUMPKIN PUDDING PIE
with cinnamon & ginger

SERVES 10
PREP 10 MINS, plus cooling
and chilling
COOK 30 MINS

10oz (300g) **vegan gingernut
cookies** (about 3 cups broken
cookies)
4 tbsp melted **plant-based butter**
or **coconut oil**
2 tsp **sea salt**
4 tbsp **instant tapioca**, such
as Minute Tapioca
1 tsp **ground cinnamon**
½ tsp **ground ginger**
¾ cup **light brown sugar**
1 cup **coconut milk coffee creamer**
1 cup **unsweetened
almond milk**
1 tbsp **maple syrup**
1 tsp **vanilla extract**
4 tbsp **cornstarch**
1 × 15oz (425g) can **pumpkin
purée**

1 Preheat the oven to 350°F (180°C). In a food processor fitted with a
metal blade, process the gingernut cookies, butter, and 1 teaspoon
of the sea salt until the mixture resembles coarse crumbs. Press this
into a deep 10in (25cm) pie dish, place the dish on a baking sheet, and
bake for 20 minutes. Remove from the oven and set aside to cool.

2 Meanwhile, in a medium saucepan, whisk together the instant
tapioca, cinnamon, ginger, brown sugar, and remaining sea salt.
Place the pan on the stove, set the heat to low, and slowly whisk in the
coconut milk coffee creamer, half of the almond milk, maple syrup, and
vanilla extract. Increase the heat to medium and bring to a boil.

3 In a small bowl, whisk together the cornstarch and remaining almond
milk. Whisk this mixture into the tapioca mixture and continue
whisking slowly for about 3 minutes or until the mixture has thickened.

4 Whisk in the pumpkin purée, remove from the heat, and cool for
10 minutes.

5 Pour the pumpkin pudding into the baked cookie crust, spreading
with a spatula to smooth the top. Cool for 10 minutes, cover with
plastic wrap (or invert a large glass bowl over the top), and refrigerate
overnight. Store any leftover pie in the refrigerator for up to 2 days.

APPLE PIE
with streusel topping

SERVES 8
PREP 25 MINS, plus cooling
COOK 1 HR

1 cup **whole-wheat flour**

1 cup **walnuts**

½ cup **light brown sugar**

2½ tsp **ground cinnamon**

4 tbsp chilled **plant-based butter**, cut into small cubes

pkg of store-bought **vegan shortcrust pastry** or **vegan prepared pastry crust**

1 cup **granulated sugar**

1 tbsp **instant tapioca**, such as Minute Tapioca

7 **apples**, such as Granny Smith, about 2lb (900g) in total, peeled, cored, and thinly sliced

juice of 1 **lemon**

1 Preheat the oven to 350°F (180°C). In a food processor fitted with a metal blade, pulse together the whole-wheat flour, walnuts, brown sugar, and ½ teaspoon of the cinnamon to combine. Add the plant-based butter and pulse until the mixture resembles coarse crumbs. Set this streusel topping aside.

2 Roll the pastry for the bottom crust into a 13in (33cm) circle and transfer to a deep 10in (25cm) pie dish. You'll have a 1in (2.5cm) overhang; fold up the overhanging dough, pinch into a rim, and use your fingers to crimp the crust. Refrigerate the pastry crust while you make the filling.

3 In a large bowl, whisk together the remaining cinnamon, granulated sugar, and instant tapioca. Add the sliced apples and lemon juice, and toss well to combine. Pour the apple mixture into the prepared pastry crust.

4 Using your hands, pick up small handfuls of the streusel topping, press into large crumbs, and break into smaller crumbs as you sprinkle it over the apple filling. Continue, covering the top of the pie evenly, until all the streusel has been used.

5 Put the pie dish on a baking sheet and bake in the lower third of the oven for about 1 hour or until the streusel topping is golden and the filling is bubbling. Check the pie once or twice during baking, and place a piece of aluminum foil over the top if the streusel starts to become too brown. Cool the pie at room temperature for 3 hours before slicing.

the good stuff

Walnuts are a good source of the essential fatty acid omega-3, which has benefits for brain health and function. They also contain vital iron for vegans, as well as selenium, zinc, vitamin E, and some B vitamins.

FEEL-GOOD CHOCOLATE MOUSSE
with cacao & avocados

SERVES 4
PREP 5 MINS, plus chilling

5 ripe **avocados**, about 2⅔ cups,
  roughly chopped
⅔ cup **raw cacao powder**
4 tbsp **maple syrup**
1 tsp **vanilla extract**
4 tbsp **almond** or **coconut milk**
cacao nibs, to serve

1 To make the mousse, place all the ingredients except the cacao nibs into a food processor and process them until completely smooth, adding a little extra almond or coconut milk if necessary.

2 Pour the mixture into a serving dish or individual 5fl oz (150ml) glasses. Refrigerate for at least 1 hour, until chilled. To serve, sprinkle the mousse with cacao nibs.

VARIATION

Try stirring through the zest of 1 orange or a teaspoon of strong filtered coffee. You could also top with finely chopped fresh mango, chopped pistachios, or pomegranate seeds.

the good stuff

These little pots have all the richness of a decadent mousse but without the cream, butter, and processed sugar. Raw cacao contains up to four times more antioxidants than regular cocoa powder.

SUMMER PUDDING
with fresh berries

SERVES 6
PREP 15 MINS, plus chilling
COOK 3–4 MINS

2lb (900g) **mixed soft fruits,**
 raspberries, strawberries,
 blackberries, pitted cherries,
 or **blueberries**
¼ cup **fructose** (fruit sugar)
8–10 thick slices of day-old
 white bread
2 tbsp **redcurrants**, to decorate
2 tbsp **mint leaves**, to decorate

1 Place the fruit in a saucepan with the fructose and 3 tablespoons of water. Heat gently and cook for 3–4 minutes or until the juices begin to run from the fruit. Set aside to cool.

2 Remove the crusts from the bread. Cut a circle from 1 slice of bread to fit the bottom of a 1-quart pudding basin or mixing bowl. Arrange the remaining bread, apart from 2 slices, around the sides of the container, overlapping slightly and leaving no gaps. Place the circle of bread over the gap at the bottom of the container.

3 Spoon the fruit mixture, together with enough juice to moisten the bread, into the container. Reserve the remaining juice. Seal in the fruit with a final layer of the remaining bread, trimming to fit as necessary.

4 Cover the pudding with a small plate or saucer and place a heavy weight on top. Place the pudding in the refrigerator for several hours, preferably overnight.

5 To serve, remove the weight and the plate and invert the pudding onto a large serving plate. Hold the two together and shake firmly, then carefully remove the container. Spoon the reserved juice over the pudding and decorate with the redcurrants and mint.

the good stuff

Strawberries are a great option here, as these little berries are even higher in vitamin C than oranges and blackberries. They are also a good source of vitamin K.

MATCHA PANNA COTTA
with tropical fruit salad

SERVES 4
PREP 25 MINS, plus cooling
and chilling
COOK 10 MINS

2 cups **coconut milk**
1 × ⅕oz (6.5g) pkg of **vegetarian
powdered setting agent**
2 tbsp **light soft brown sugar**
½ tsp **matcha powder**
1 tbsp **sunflower oil**

FRUIT SALAD
1 **passion fruit**
½ **ripe mango**, peeled
and finely diced
1 **ripe kiwi**, finely diced
½ **ripe papaya**, peeled
and finely diced

1 Transfer 3 tablespoons of the coconut milk into a medium heat-resistant bowl. Scatter the setting agent over the surface of the milk and whisk it in well, then leave to rest for 5 minutes. Meanwhile, heat the remaining coconut milk in a small, heavy-based saucepan over low heat until it is hot but not boiling.

2 When the coconut milk is hot, remove it from the heat and pour it over the setting agent mixture, whisking well to ensure that all the powder has dissolved. Whisk in the brown sugar and matcha powder until completely combined.

3 Rub the insides of 4 5fl oz (150ml) ramekins with a piece of paper towel dipped in the sunflower oil. Divide the coconut mixture among the ramekins and allow the mixture to cool before transferring to the refrigerator for at least 4–6 hours, until set.

4 To make the fruit salad, cut the passion fruit in half and scrape the seeds out into a bowl. Mix the diced mango, kiwi, and papaya with the passion fruit seeds and set aside.

5 To serve the panna cottas, fill a bowl with hot water and carefully dip the outside of each ramekin briefly into the water to loosen the panna cotta, being careful not to allow the water to drip onto the set cream. Run a small knife around the edge of the panna cotta and turn out onto individual serving plates. Serve with the fruit salad.

the good stuff

This dairy-free panna cotta is flavored with matcha powder, which contains an amino acid called theanine that may help to keep you mentally alert. Mango, kiwi, and papaya provide antioxidants and natural sweetness.

BANANA OAT COOKIES
with chocolate chips

MAKES 16
PREP 15 MINS
COOK 12–14 MINS

1 medium very ripe
   banana, peeled
⅔ cup **granulated sugar**
⅓ cup **light brown sugar**
⅓ cup **grapeseed oil**
1 tsp **vanilla extract**
1 cup **all-purpose flour**
1¾ cups **rolled oats**
½ tsp **baking soda**
½ tsp **ground cinnamon**
¼ tsp **sea salt**
⅓ cup **vegan dark**
   chocolate chips
4 tbsp **unsweetened**
   dried coconut

1 Preheat the oven to 350°F (180°C). Line 2 baking sheets with parchment paper.

2 In a medium bowl, mash the banana with the sugars, grapeseed oil, and vanilla extract until smooth.

3 Stir the flour, rolled oats, baking soda, cinnamon, sea salt, dark chocolate chips, and coconut into the banana mixture, using your hands to ensure the mixture is well combined. It will be very thick.

4 Scoop 1½in (3.75cm) balls of dough onto the baking sheets, spacing them about 2½in (6cm) apart. Using wet hands, gently pat down the cookies into 2in (5cm) rounds. Some chocolate chips might separate from the mixture; if they do, just pat them back into the cookies.

5 Bake for 12–14 minutes or until the cookies are golden. Cool for 3 minutes on the baking sheets, then transfer to a wire rack to cool completely. The cookies will keep in an airtight container for up to 5 days (if they last that long!).

the good stuff

Oats are a real supergrain. They contain beta-glucans, a soluble fiber that slows down the absorption of carbs into the bloodstream, which discourages our bodies from making and storing fat.

flex it

If you're not vegan and you're
not a fan of dark chocolate,
just swap the chips for milk
chocolate ones.

MANGO YOGURT ICE
with lime zest

SERVES 4
PREP 5 MINS, plus cooling
  and freezing
COOK 2 MINS

3 ripe **mangoes**, about
  8oz (225g) each
1 cup **powdered sugar**
zest and juice of 1 **lime**
4 tbsp **plant-based yogurt**

1 Extract as much fruit as you can from the mangoes, using a knife to scrape the pulp from the skin and pit. Discard the skin and pit and place the pulp in a liquid measuring cup. You should have around 1¾ cups.

2 In a small saucepan, gently heat the powdered sugar and ½ cup of water, and stir until the sugar is dissolved (about 2 minutes). Cool to room temperature. This makes around ¾ cup of syrup.

3 In a food processor, blend together the mango pulp, syrup, lime zest and juice, and the yogurt.

4 Place in an ice-cream maker and churn and freeze according to the manufacturer's instructions. Before serving, remove from the freezer and put in the refrigerator for 20 minutes to soften.

RHUBARB SORBET
with lemon

SERVES 6
PREP 20 MINS, plus
   cooling and freezing
COOK 10 MINS

juice of 1 large **lemon**
1¼ cups **powdered sugar**
1lb (450g) **rhubarb**
   chopped into 1in
   (2.5cm) pieces
2 tbsp **glucose syrup**

1 Place 1 cup of water, lemon juice, and powdered sugar in a saucepan. Over low heat, stir until the sugar dissolves.

2 Add the rhubarb, bring to a boil, and simmer for 8 minutes or until the rhubarb is pulpy. Cool to room temperature.

3 Transfer the mixture to a food processor and purée until completely smooth. Stir in the glucose syrup, pulsing briefly for about 25 seconds.

4 Place in an ice-cream maker and churn and freeze according to the manufacturer's instructions. Remove from the freezer 10 minutes before serving.

the good stuff

Eating rhubarb is good for your well-being. Vegans don't naturally have as much calcium in their diets as those who eat dairy, but rhubarb provides a good supply of this essential nutrient to promote strong bones and teeth.

CHOCOLATE LAYER CAKE
with fresh berries

SERVES 10
PREP 30 MINS
COOK 40 MINS

2¾ cups **all-purpose flour**

3⅓ cups **powdered sugar**

1¾ tsp **baking soda**

⅔ cup **vegan cocoa powder**

¼ tsp **salt**

2 cups **unsweetened soy milk**
   or **water**

½ cup **corn** or **vegetable oil**, plus
   extra for greasing

1½ tbsp **white vinegar**

1½ tsp **vanilla extract**

GANACHE

10oz (300g) **vegan dark chocolate**

1¼ cups **plant-based milk**

TO DECORATE

1½oz (45g) **vegan chocolate**,
   shaved with a potato peeler, or
   a selection of **fresh berries**, if
   preferred

1 Preheat the oven to 350°F (180°C). Grease and line with parchment paper the bases of 2 deep 8in (20cm) round layer cake pans.

2 Sift together into a large bowl the flour, powdered sugar, baking soda, cocoa powder, and salt. In a separate bowl, mix together the liquid ingredients: the soy milk or water, corn oil, white vinegar, and vanilla extract, and add to the flour mixture. Stir until smooth.

3 Divide the mixture between the prepared pans, and use a palette knife or spatula to spread evenly. Bake in the oven for about 40 minutes, until risen and firm to the touch.

4 Cool in the pans for 10 minutes, then turn out onto a wire rack, remove the parchment paper, and leave to cool completely. Slice each cake in half horizontally.

5 To make the ganache, melt the dark chocolate and combine with the plant-based milk.

6 Sandwich the cakes together using half the ganache for the first 3 layers. Spread the remainder on the top and sides and rough up with a knife. Sprinkle with chocolate shavings or decorate with fresh berries, if you'd like.

POMEGRANATE & RASPBERRY GRANITA
with fresh mint

SERVES 8
PREP 20 MINS, plus freezing

2¼lb (1kg) **seedless watermelon**
  (about 1½ mini watermelons) or
  ½ large watermelon, skinned
  and diced
1½ cups **raspberries**,
  plus extra to decorate
1⅛ cups **pomegranate seeds**,
  plus extra to decorate
large handful of **mint leaves**,
  plus extra to decorate
1–2 tbsp **maple syrup**

1 Place half the watermelon in a blender or food processor, along with half the raspberries, pomegranate seeds, and mint leaves. Process to a liquid and pour into a large bowl. Blend the remaining watermelon, raspberries, pomegranate seeds, and mint, and combine with the first batch of liquid. (Working in batches prevents the blender or food processor from overflowing.)

2 Put the resulting liquid through a fine metal sieve and strain into a large bowl, pressing down with the back of a spoon to extract all the liquid from the pulp. Discard the pulp. If you are using seeded watermelon, also discard any fragments of seed.

3 Whisk in the maple syrup as needed, depending on the sweetness of the watermelon. Remember that the sweetness will be dulled on freezing, so adjust according to your taste.

4 Pour the liquid into a large, freezerproof airtight container and freeze. Remove from the freezer every 2 hours and use a metal fork to scrape the frozen sides back into the granita, crushing the resulting crystals as you go. Repeat three times, until it is completely frozen.

5 Remove from the freezer and put in the refrigerator for 30 minutes before serving. To serve, scrape out layers of crystals into individual serving bowls or glasses and garnish with extra raspberries, pomegranate seeds, and mint leaves.

the good stuff

This fresh-tasting granita is a simple superfood and dairy-free alternative to ice cream and doesn't require an ice-cream maker. It's packed with antioxidant pomegranates, vitamin C-rich raspberries, and immune-boosting mint.

BERRY & LIME MUNG BEAN ICE POPS
with sweet agave nectar

MAKES 10
PREP 20 MINS, plus freezing

1½ cups **blueberries**
1½ cups **blackberries**
⅓ cup cooked **mung beans**
3 tbsp **lime juice**
⅓ cup **agave nectar**

1 In a blender or food processor, purée the blueberries, blackberries, mung beans, lime juice, agave nectar, and ⅓ cup of water until completely smooth.

2 Pour the mixture through a fine sieve to remove the seeds. Press the mixture against the sieve to retain as much liquid as possible.

3 Pour the liquid into 10 ice pop molds. Insert a stick into each mold. Freeze for at least 6 hours or overnight before serving.

VARIATION

For a flavor variation, swap the berries for raspberries and strawberries. For a taste of the tropics, use fresh pineapple and mango.

the good stuff

These make the perfect low-calorie treat. Mung beans are packed with vitamin B6, which supports adrenal function and helps to calm and maintain a healthy nervous system. Agave nectar is a great vegan alternative to honey.

INDEX

Pantry ingredients in the recipes such as flour or flavorings are not included in this index. Herbs or spices in large amounts are included.

ACKNOWLEDGMENTS

Material in this publication was first published in Great Britain in *Allergy-Free Cookbook* (2007), *The Cooking Book* (2008), *The Diabetes Cookbook* (2010), *The More Veg Cookbook* (2013), *Mediterranean Cookbook* (2014), *Grains as Mains* (2015), *Plant Based Cookbook* (2016), *Superfood Breakfasts* (2016), *Power Bowls* (2016), *Energy Bites* (2016), *Power Pulses* (2017), *Super Clean Super Foods* (2017), *100 Weight Loss Bowls* (2017), and *Sprouted* (2017).

All photography and artworks © Dorling Kindersley

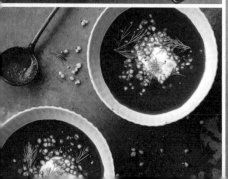